MW01295093

Then is Now

**READING THE NEW TESTAMENT IN THE
21ST CENTURY**

Rev Wayne R Viereck

ISBN: 1543274714

ISBN 13: 9781543274714

Library of Congress Control Number: 2017905125

CreateSpace Independent Publishing Platform

North Charleston, South Carolina

Dedication

Why this book? Why did I write this book? While I have a Master's degree in Theology, and a doctorate in Ministry, I am neither a theologian nor a textual scholar. I have been a Parish Pastor for the past fifty-five years, and still today. This requires me to wrestle with the texts of the New Testament, and while I seldom if ever defeat them (I have been thrown to the mat more often than not), I do not come away from the confrontation so much bloodied, as chastened and empowered. (Sometimes bloodied!) I try to apply that experience to the sermons and studies and conversation which make up life in my community of faith.

More times than I can remember, reactions to those sermons and studies, and the substance of those conversations, has been a sharing of the doubt, the uncertainty, the fear and hope which is unavoidable for a follower of Jesus in the current world. So often the concerns expressed in those conversations, are the ones I deal with in this little book. The sense of relief when someone has said, "I don't have to take that literally?" and the true joy in the Lord which has broken through in times of mortal doubt and ethical dilemma, for which I have been allowed by the Spirit to be the means through which understanding has come, has been blessing beyond any kind of deserving.

Those experiences, of grace, and love and breakthrough spirituality, are the background to, and the reason for this book. I have preached and taught what is contained herein for more than fifty years and in that time have witnessed the power of the Gospel to bring life and new life, hope and resolve and amazing works of love and charity.

So I enter this task in thankful appreciation for the fellowship and growth in faith, and for the understanding of the New Testament shared with me by the communities of faith in which I have been blessed to live the Good News of what God has done in our Lord Christ:

Grace Lutheran Church, Woodstock, Illinois
Shepherd of the Hill Lutheran Church, Lockport, Illinois
St Timothy's Lutheran Church, Skokie, Illinois
St. Mark Lutheran Church, Rockford, Illinois
Fox Point Church Lutheran Church, Fox Point, Wisconsin
The Community Church, SaddleBrooke Arizona
Resurrection Lutheran Church, Tucson, Arizona

Most of all, I am able to do this little book because of the love and encouragement given to me by my wife, my editor and reviewer. Thanks be to God for Pat, my greatest blessing!

Wayne Viereck
Tucson Arizona
2017

Table of Contents

Then is Now

One overriding question must be addressed before we venture into the texts and teachings of the New Testament itself. Does it really matter what we believe or just that we believe "'something" beyond ourselves? Are all religious views ultimately acceptable because we are all on the same road to God, or is it possible that some religious understanding is more accurate than others; and is it possible that some might even be wrong? This is a concern for all of us; we want to be right, and, especially in the ultimate issue of what we believe, we do not want to follow false or misleading viewpoints. We want to be sure, certain, and right in what we believe. After all, we think our eternal life may depend upon it!

The possibility of ever possessing certainty in what is "right" is demolished for us however even in a quick reading of history. It shows that, as human life moves on through the centuries, the simple fact of living brings changes in world view, scientific, cultural and theological understanding; and the "to die for" insight of one generation becomes merely a marginal gloss or footnote for the next. Every age has its own new ideas and concorns, every generation its "great new thing;" and it always seems to those caught up in that fantastic new insight that it is a revolution in thought and understanding never known before.

It seems it always has been this way and likely will continue to be this way. But if that is true, it rather quickly leads us into a crisis of confusion. How can we ever know what to believe, how can we be sure that what is being taught right now is the "real truth" and not just the current perspective, which could well change with new or better information to-morrow? Is there a real and irreducible honest-to-goodness reality that we can believe in and hold on to, a "rock of ages," "a "little brown church in the vale," a core truth that will not change, does not change, ever? How can we know it is so? How can we know anything is really "so"?

Those on the conservative end of the theological spectrum tell us the New Testament is the rock of ages we are seeking. Then we discover the New Testament says many things, some of them seem impossible to believe, and for many this whole approach and perspective is ultimately judged to be inadequate. Those on the more liberal end of the faith fair no better, telling us "it is impossible to understand the New Testament without theological interpretation," which only raises the question of "whose interpretation?" making that answer also very inadequate. The temptation is to throw up our hands, just close the book, put it on the shelf and forget it. Alternatively, just accept the teachings of "The Church" or whomever we choose to go along with.

This book is written in the belief that the New Testament continues to be viable, true and life changing in the 21st century, when it is read with respect to the culture of the age in which it was written. It is the central premise of this book that, in the truest sense, to understand the New Testament, we must bring "then" into "now," recapture the imagination we had as a little child, that openness to the possibility that anything could be. Only by giving up a literal and linear reading of the text can the metaphoric and symbolic images in which the New Testament was writ-ten once again become real for us. We need to read the text of scripture and let it speak to us in its own way. When Jesus speaks to Zacchaeus, hear him speaking to you; put yourself in the crowd that hears and watch-es, and let your imagination take over.

When we read the New Testament, it is an experience which is all about us. We are being addressed; the Spirit is speaking to us; so we must put ourselves into the story. It must become our story in the same way as when I read the story of Cinderella to my granddaughter and for that moment she was Cinderella. That is the way of a child perhaps, but that is also the way to read the Bible. No one comes to understand his or her relationship to God through contemplation or philosophical discussion. That happens only when we enter into the story of what God has done as the New Testament presents it, getting into the story ourselves, speaking the parts, taking the role of the characters. Be the Pharisee; be the sinner; be the woman; and hear what Jesus is saying to you. Nevertheless, while we are taking the story personally, we are hearing it and living the results of our hearing, within the community of faith we call the church, the community that shapes our faith and nourishes it. Within the community we strive to live in the spirit of God-- to love as we are loved, to forgive as we are forgiven--which is what Jesus called taking up our cross and following him.

But if Jesus could not carry that cross alone, we certainly cannot. We need each other, and we need the community of faith. And, the thrust of this book, we also need the community of faith to rightly read the New Testament in the 21st century, or any century, for the New Testament was written by the community of faith for the community of faith. And, within the community, the faith of the first believers still resonates, uplifts and testifies, so that in the truest sense, "Then is Now!"

Part One

*The Historical Setting
to the New Testament*

Chapter One

The Risk of Reading the New Testament

As we turn to the New Testament, we must admit that we live in the 21st century and bring the worldview of our time and place, as well as our own life experiences, into our confrontation with it. That is good; the New Testament can stand up to that. We do not have to sanitize our expectations or meet a set of criterion to properly interpret it, but we do have to meet it on its own terms. We have to let the New Testament be the New Testament. No one would expect a history book to give recipes for cookies, or to be a primer on biology, or list the stats of players in the NFL. That's a silly example, to be sure; yet people do bring similar kinds of expectations to the New Testament and then are disappointed when it doesn't meet them. However, the New Testament does not answer every question we bring to it; it is neither a rulebook nor an answer book for a God-pleasing life. It certainly did not fall from heaven all ready to read; there is a process to the development of the New Testament and to a large extent, it is a very human process.

Our biggest problem with Scripture is that everyone regards it as a Holy Book ...the word of God ...but they don't read it. Many have said "It's too difficult," resulting in a plethora of "easier" translations and para-phrases, designed to make it less difficult. Yet it remains too hard to read because what is really meant is not that the translations are too hard (reading the King James Version is not that much more difficult than more contemporary translations); what is meant is that it seems simply outside of our reality. There is so much strange stuff: if your right hand sins, cut it off; a woman who commits adultery shall be put to death; give away all you possess, etc. And then, when we seek answers to specific questions: "What does the Bible say about homosexuality, death with dignity, abortion, "we discover that people read the same texts and come away with totally different answers.

It has been attributed to Martin Luther, but it was a wise person who said, "Read the Bible seriously but not literally." Ok, but what does "seriously" mean? Everyone takes the Scripture seriously, but many also take it literally. It would be nice if we could, with integrity and honesty, take the Bible literally. If every word were the word of God fallen from heaven to be read and understood just as it is, then we could read it and know exactly what God is saying to us. There is a great hunger for that kind of certainty; and the more complicated things in the world become, the more we want an undoubted authority to tell us what the right thing is.

If only we COULD say, "The Bible says... and so that's that!" But the most fundamental assertion the Bible makes is that God has created us with the freedom--and the responsibility--to adapt, adjust, and decide for ourselves. An awesome thing, it is sometimes a joy, sometimes a burden; but that is what it means to be a child of God, not a slave of God. Every parent wants his or her child to come to the right decisions; but sometimes, as we see our children wrestle with solutions and seem to be ready to make a mistake, we would just like to tell them what that right decision would be. I hope that we don't, because not a one of us would want our children to simply do everything we tell them; we want them to be persons in their own right. God gives that same freedom to us; and when it comes to reading God's Word, living in freedom means that since we are not slaves, we should not read God's word "slavishly." We must come to the Bible with our whole person, all that we are, not suspending our critical faculties or simply believing and not doubting. But, coming as we are, bringing all that we are, means we come willing to take the risk that reading the Bible brings with it.

It's a double risk really...

The first risk is that God might really break through to us, might change us; for when we really open ourselves to God's word and listen, we might not like what we hear. Many who heard Jesus "then" did not like what they heard. Many do not like it "now" either, and some of the reason the Bible is considered to be too hard is that what it says is sometimes too pointed for us to hear, and even harder to accept; so we put it aside, not because it's too difficult, but because it is just too uncomfortable.

The second risk is that we might break through to God. The New Testament becomes the word of God when we come with open hearts, seeking a conversation with God in which we can ask, doubt, criticize, question. Abraham argued with God and we too should feel free to say, "That can't be true! That is stupid! What a dumb point of view." God's word takes us seriously as a person and asks us to take his word seriously as well, and that is why reading the Bible is "so hard!"

When we take that risk, when we open ourselves to a real and honest conversation, we may break through to God and God may break through to us, and a miracle may take place. The love and grace of God may embrace us, and the fear and resistance within us may melt away, and we may find ourselves saying with Jacob of old "Surely the Lord was here, and I did not know it." It is my hope that this little book will help us to take that risk and put aside our reluctance to enter that conversation.

Our jaded and cynical world has told us the New Testament is no longer credible in a 21st century world. Nothing could be further from the truth, but to read the New Testament we must we bring to our reading the very same human honesty and openness the writers brought to writing it.

The New Testament was created by a very human process in which the writers were involved with every level of their being. To read it requires the same from the reader. The New Testament is a human creation, and it was written within a very human history. Yet we would have to believe in a series of incredible coincidences to maintain it is ONLY a human process at work. To that story, we turn next.

Chapter Two

It all begins with the Hebrew Scriptures

As we begin our look at the New Testament from a 21st century perspective, it is crucially important to remember that it is rooted in, and derives from, the Old Testament. The Gospels are actually the final link in a long process of recounting God's activity in the world, first within the community of faith of the Jews, and then with the followers of Jesus. The new Christian community was born within what we call the Old Testament, or Hebrew Scriptures.

Scholars prefer the term Hebrew Scriptures, or Hebrew Bible, rather than Old Testament, in order to avoid being insensitive to Jews, for whom it is not the Old Testament but God's Word to the people of the covenant, still "new," still valid, still the current word of God. I appreciate that, and agree with it. Yet the title is equally a sensitive matter for Christians, for to call the Old Testament the Hebrew Scriptures undercuts the Christian understanding that, while God was at work in and throughout the life and history of the Jews, it was to bring about the day of the Messiah, whom Christians know to be Jesus of Nazareth.

The New Testament makes no sense if it is divorced from the action of God in the life of the Jews before the coming of Jesus. The German scholars created a term for this, "Heilsgeschichte" which means "salvation history," a seamless blending of both Testaments into a complete story of God's intrusion into the world to bring salvation--through the

Jews, through Jesus, for all people. Whether we call it Old Testament or Hebrew Scripture, it is the salvation story for Jew and Christian alike, the Gospels presenting the story of Jesus as the fulfillment of the prophetic promises; he is the Messiah long awaited.

The Gospels and Old Testament are basically composed in the same manner and use the same storytelling methods; so to better understand how the Gospels were written, we will take a look at how the Hebrew Scripture was written. Both Testaments are a collection of prayers, poems, stories, liturgies, sermons, letters, sayings, and other forms of oral and written communication. These were collected, edited, reworked and reused, primarily to witness and proclaim to others, but equally for use in the daily events and ever-new situations of life in the community of faith. Both the Hebrew Scripture and the New Testament are the products of years of oral and written processes shared and repeated in the community, often for generations, before being finally finished in written form.

I must first disavow any understanding of the nuances and sophisticated differences in understanding among the divisions within Judaism. That is a study beyond my ability. However, for purpose of illustration, of how the Hebrew Scripture and New Testament are the products of the community of faith, the following is a Cliff Notes version, but accurate enough for our purpose, which is not the Hebrew Scripture but the New Testament.

Jewish and Christian scholars hold differences of opinion regarding how God's revelation occurred within the community but are in complete agreement that, in whatever manner it happened, both Testaments are a product of men and women of faith experiencing the presence of God within their lives and within the life of the community. The oral tradition regarding Jesus existed before the Gospels, and in much the same way the first five books of the Hebrew Scripture existed in oral form before being written down. This is not to say that writing was unknown in the ancient world. Egyptian Hieroglyphs were in use by 3200 B.C.E., and Cuneiform, a pictograph type of writing, developed by the Sumerians at least as early as Egyptian Hieroglyphs, was in wide use by 2800 B.C.E.

There is archaeological evidence of Hebrew writing in Jerusalem as early as 1000 B.C.E, but it was not until the return from Babylonian exile about 540 B.C.E, that we have definitive written record of the books which comprise the Hebrew Scriptures. There may have been older written texts but none have survived, and it is widely assumed that the nomadic tribes of Israel were largely an oral culture.

This likely assumption becomes clear to us as we read the stories of those first books--about what Abraham did, how Isaac did this or that, what happened to Joseph, the exile time in Egypt, etc. It is history abbreviated into personalities, which made it much easier for an oral culture to remember. Much more happened during that long time period, but from the faith standpoint of the community, what happened to Abraham and Isaac, Joseph and the family, shows how God was involved in their lives. It is Hebrew History, but it is also the story of God's love and concern for all his people.

Much of the Old Testament began in oral story and tradition; and when putting it into written form, the author often became an editor as well, because he was required to choose between different strains or versions of the same story. Over years of telling, the stories did somewhat change, but the high regard they had in the community prevented significant change; so when the editor confronted different accounts of events, rather than choosing between them, he simply included them all in his writing--one after the other, or blended together, or sometimes placing one of them into a new context.

As we read the Hebrew Scripture, we notice how often the same story is told in different ways. A good example of this is the creation story in Genesis. 1:1-2:3 is the first account of creation, a complete story beautifully told. But then, 2:4 starts the whole story over again; thus Genesis presents two creation accounts woven together, the joining together very clear even in English translation. While in many ways the accounts are complementary, each giving different details, it is quite clear they are two different versions of the same story. Scholars call the first account the "J" version, compiled in the 9th century B.C.E. The second account is termed the "P" version compiled in the 7th century B.C.E. These two versions were independent accounts of creation until combined during the Babylonian exile, possibly as a Hebrew answer to the various creation accounts in the myths of the Babylonians, among whom the exiled Jews lived.

Both Genesis stories are what scholars call an "origin story," that is, they intend to explain the origin of the earth and humanity. Other origin stories deal with how the rainbow came into existence (the flood story), or why there are so many languages in the world (the tower of Babel story). Scholars call origin stories "myth," but they do not mean that term in the sense of classical literature's myths of the gods of Rome and Greece. Origin stories are not historical, and by their very nature are beyond historical verification, but they are still true. They are truth in the highest and deepest sense; poetic truth, existential truth, a spiritual truth which lies at the most profound level of existence.

The story of Adam and Eve, an origin story telling how human life came to be, is a good example of this. It is not a story of an historical event from a time far back in the dawn of history; it is the story of every human being. It is my story, your story; because the point is to tell us that we are Adam or Eve. The real intention of the story of Adam and Eve is not to be a history lesson, but a theology lesson. It does not tell us historical truth about two people, but existential truth about all people. It tells us who we are, and why we are, that our life originated in a creative act of God, that we are God's personally created children intended to live in intimate relationship with God. And the story tells us something else about ourselves--we are self-centered disobedient people, who break our relationship with God and with each other; and because disobedience has consequences, we have troubles, pain and death. The book of Genesis contains many origin stories about the deepest and most basic human questions ..."Who am I? Why is there evil? Why do we die? "

The creation story in Genesis answers in a beautiful way that "God did it," and the stories of the tower of Babel, the flood, Noah's ark, the walls of Jericho, while not historical in the sense that they "actually happened," are metaphors which tell us truth on a much deeper level of reality than actual history could ever do. Of course, not all the stories in the Hebrew Scriptures are origin stories or metaphors, much **is** history in our common definition of the word, recording events and dates which actually happened and can be historically verified; Hezekiah was King, Jeremiah was a prophet, and so on.

As we move to the New Testament, the concern of this book, we must keep in mind that the Old Testament was the only Scripture the early community had. It was God's word to them, and they understood the new faith in Jesus as a fulfillment, or completion, of what God had been leading up to throughout that long history of the Jewish people. The New Testament was, as Matthew put it repeatedly, "This was done to fulfill the scripture ...."

Chapter Three

Myths and Metaphors

There are many ways to read the Bible, all of them have their place, yet some are more true to the purpose and intention of the New Testament witness than others; and some will get you into downright impossible situations. This book proposes a way to read the New Testament in the 21st century, not the 18th century or the 10th century. The people of other centuries were people of their time, just as we are people of our time; and neither they nor we are able to understand truth and reality, or even philosophize about them, except that we must do it within the culture and science of our time and place. This is termed a "worldview." We will look at the changing worldview of the western church during the past 2000 years, and how it affected the understanding of the New Testament, from the 1st century to the 21st.

The composition of the New Testament can be compared to the plumbing in our homes. Not many of us are deeply interested in the plumbing; we just want the water to be there when we turn the faucet. Still it is important that we have at least an understanding that to get the water to where we want it there are pipes, which connect to water mains, which ultimately connect us to a well or the water supply. Not to know that is to be subject to crazy theories of how the water gets to the faucet. So also in regard to reading the New Testament, not to realize that the word of the Lord comes to us through some ancient well laid pipes will lead to crazy theories and get us into some impossible situations. We will look at the plumbing behind the New Testament, not in scholarly detail, but enough to give us an appreciation of what a truly incredible gift it is and how, in a deeper sense than we ever imagined, the Bible **is** the word of God. And, then is now!

In order to capture the wonder of the events they were relating, those New Testament pipes were laid by authors who made extensive use of metaphor, hyperbole, poetry, and other literary devices. A metaphor is an image that suggests something else, a myth is a metaphor, and both are a form of poetry which attempts to understand mystery; through a sophisticated relating of the deepest realities which are inexpressible in any other manner

As the gospel authors created a metaphor, they knew the experience itself was real, even as they knew the metaphor or myth through which they were relating the experience was not real, in a physically measurable sense. The metaphors of the New Testament were never intended to be understood in a literal manner for they were expressing something beyond literal explanation. A metaphor is poetic explanation; it is spiritual explanation. As the authors related their own personal experience and that of others within the community, they did so in a manner close to Carl Jung's "Collective Unconscious" (more recently termed "objective psyche"). Of course, they did not know the theories of Jung, but they knew the reality of Jung's position: that all human beings share an innate and common understanding of myth and metaphor. He termed them "archetypes," the shared human understanding of the image of city, death, hero, mother and so on. Jung maintained that all human beings understand such metaphors and myths.

Matthew, Mark, Luke and John used myth and metaphor in just that manner; tapping into the universal understanding of poetic images and myths as the means to express the reality they experienced in the ministry of Jesus and in their experience of his resurrection. They wrote knowing they would be understood on the level of deepest truth, their meaning and intention not limited to the literal words they had to use. As they selected from the oral tradition, edited it, and directed it to a particular audience, it was a conscious and deliberate process. Moreover, throughout its 2000-year history, the church has done the same thing, understanding the Bible from constantly changing viewpoints. In the second century allegorical methods were popular in dealing with difficult situations or problems raised by the text. In the 19th century Thomas Jefferson famously simply cut out of the New Testament those portions with which he did not agree. In less drastic but similar manner, some simply ignore that with which they do not agree. Others take even the most difficult passages literally.

None of those approaches are viable in the twenty-first century, for they ignore the fact that, in the deepest sense, reading the New Testament is a sacramental experience; it mediates to us the living God, who speaks to our present situation of life, both personally and within the community of faith we call the "Church." The New Testament is God's word not because it is a divine composition (although it most certainly is), but because when we enter into dialog with it, the New Testament becomes God's word to us. The Holy Spirit works within the community in a dialogic manner, that is, within a dialog between the believer and the Spirit-- sometimes confrontational, sometimes comforting--but always personal and directly addressed to our life situation.

While this sacramental understanding may seem a new paradigm, it is really the most ancient and original understanding of Christianity and of the New Testament. In the earliest days of the faith, while detours from time to time took the church down paths that proved to be dead ends-- such as insisting faith meant believing the right dogma, doing the right things, or living in the right way--the essence of the faith always remained strongly centered on a personal experience of the Spirit. Always it was a responding to the call of the Holy Spirit, accepting the love and forgiveness offered in Jesus, and then living with God and the people of God in a relationship that begins in this life and never ends.

This was the message of the Christian faith within the early community. Then, as the church moved into the secular world, it adopted, and then adapted, much of the secular worldview. To give just one example, it was necessary to establish a form of administration to bring order to the rapidly growing community. The model of the Roman Empire, so close at hand in their daily life, became the model for the church. As good as this idea seemed at the time, the unintended and unexpected result was a shifting of the original understanding of the New Testament into something quite different. It was not the choice of the Roman model alone, many factors were involved, but the community became an institution, and the personal experience of the Spirit became captive to dogma, doctrine, and an ecclesiastical power structure. To enable the development of what was to become the "orthodox" or accepted understanding, the metaphors of the Gospel authors were replaced by the view that the word of God was dictated directly to the Gospel authors. Mark, Matthew, Luke and John became merely the mechanical means through which the words were put into written form. Therefore, because God himself had spoken the words, the New Testament was inerrant and infallible and could provide the authority by which the church developed the doctrine, dogma, and creeds etc., which, ironically, would eventually relegate the New Testament to secondary role as the authority in the church!

In the 21st century that literal understanding of the New Testament is so totally shot throughout the church, that to propose a return to the earlier understanding of the New Testament, feels, looks, seems, like something entirely new! For many that will be very uncomfortable, not only because change itself is difficult to accept, but because so much has been invested in the 10th to 20th century understanding of how the New Testament should be read. The old paradigm is so ingrained we fear that to let it go means to give up the authority of the New Testament for our faith. If every word is not God's word, then how do we know which word is God's word? The fear is that, if we question the virgin birth or the ascension of Jesus as historical fact, it calls into question the validity of the whole New Testament.

No, it does not! In fact, NOT to make the 21st century paradigm shift and return to the understanding of the early church will ultimately remove all authority from the scriptures and make of it what the author Christopher Hitchens called, "... a babyish attempt to meet our inescapable demand for knowledge, as well as for comfort, reassurance, and other infantile needs." (Daniel Florien, writing in *Patheos* December 16, 2011)

But for those who have difficulty with the 10th or 18th century view of Biblical interpretation, what I call the "sacramental" understanding of the New Testament is a breath of fresh air; it is the spirit blowing through the church bringing new life to a New Testament, which had become rigid, moralistic, and dangerously close to no longer making meaningful sense. However, that is not true for all believers, and even as this new (actually old) paradigm re-emerges, the other one is still useful and valid for many, and that is fine with me. If the 20th century view works for you, why change it? As it is said, "If it's not broke don't fix it."

However, in my fifty-five years as a parish Pastor, I have learned that for many it is broke and does need fixing. Two opposing views....but there is nothing new about that! Many ways in which to understand the New Testament have been present in the church from the very beginning; and the Spirit has used them all and will continue to do so. St. Paul put it well when he said the Gospel is an obstacle to some, life and nourishment to others; and that while some of us can live on milk and mush, others require red meat. I guess that is a way of saying that whatever works for you is good for you. However, to quote St. Paul again, "I hope to show you a more excellent way." I hope to show you that in reading the New Testament, "Then is Now."

Chapter Four

Historical Situation

As we continue in our understanding of how the Bible is best read within the 21st century, the next chapters take us back into the earliest decades of what was to become the Christian church. Would that all we are about to explore was history in the popular sense of "what actually happened," but very little of either the early church or the gospel narrative is really history in that sense of the word; and when it comes to the New Testament, historical facts are few and many of them uncertain. But then, what is history? How do you write history? Aristotle said history is what so-and-so did or had done to him, presumably from so-and-so's point of view. Churchill famously said, "History is written by the victors." Henry Ford put it this way ..."History is bunk."

To the Jews of the First Century history was not bunk; it was the story of the "Mighty acts of God" at work in the world. This was equally true for the Jewish and Gentile members of the early Christian community. They believed the power of God upheld every moment of history, even though at the time it is not clear what God is about or how he is doing it; that is something which only comes clear much later, looking back. So if we want to know what God was doing in the early community, if we want to know "what actually happened" in Jesus' ministry and in the developing church, how do we do that? Is it possible to know the history of the early church?

Henry Ford is ultimately too cynical: history is not bunk, but as is true for every human endeavor, history is a compilation of confusing and often contradictory, or seemingly contradictory, facts and opinions. Yes, some of it, sometimes, is "bunk," but that is so when it does not have an organizing point of view, to make it comprehensible. Nothing can make sense in history, philosophy, physics, science, any human discipline until there is a point of view from which to arrange all the facts and guesses, the surmises and possibilities that make up historical life. Whether it is scientific theorem or Biblical interpretation, there must be a place on which to stand, a solid rock from which to say ..."This is what I see as truth, now show me differently."

The organizing principle of the New Testament is that God raised Jesus from the dead. With the experience of that previously unbelievable event firmly in place, the early Christian community looked back upon the events of Jesus' life, and from the undoubted "rock" of his resurrection, understood his life and ministry as filled with a meaning and purpose they had not previously realized. The honesty of the Gospel writers admits this in various places, as they tell us the disciples sometimes failed to understand a parable or a miracle and had to ask Jesus what it meant. However, after the resurrection they realized to a much greater extent than they had at the time, that God was indeed present within Jesus; in fact, maybe, the reason he had so often astounded them, was that he was God!

As they looked back from that high and exhilarating place, that mountaintop certainty of the resurrection, everything was filled with a new meaning, new depth and purpose. Nothing was as they had thought because God was in Jesus doing a new thing! God the creator was bringing about a new creation! The resurrection of Jesus made clear the whole reason why God had chosen the Jewish people to be the vehicle through which God would redeem the whole world. Thanks to the Spirit, now they had what Jesus had often called "eyes that see."

Let me give an everyday example of how that works. A man is accused of a crime. He said he didn't do it. The "facts" seemed to say otherwise; his wife said, "I believe in him, he didn't do it." Still he was convicted. Many years later new facts proved he did not do it. The supposed facts at the time were wrong. No, not exactly, one fact was right... his wife said he didn't do it, based upon the "truer fact" that she knew him, believed in him. She had faith in him, her faith was the rock on which she had stood, and she was right.

Of course, she could have been wrong. Faith can be misplaced. But facts can be erroneously interpreted as well. The problem of life and history is that we can never really know anything with total objective certainty. All we can know with the kind of certainty that matters is what is revealed to us, not by the facts, but by faith. Many disparage faith as being little more than self-delusion, but actually it is best defined as "trust," which while it is a subjective knowledge is one that is so much deeper than supposedly more trustworthy "objective" facts. For example, I know my wife loves me, and I know that because I see it in who she is, by who we are together, by so many levels of awareness beyond merely what she says and does. It is, so to speak, a spiritual certainty not dependent upon her deeds and actions alone.

Now, to be sure, subjective knowledge by itself, without deeds and actions, without objective proof, can lead us, as it often has, into foolish and downright ridiculous beliefs and assertions. The belief in which we trust must be solid, anchored in reality. In terms of reading the Bible in the 21st century this means that personal interpretation must be subject to the experience of the whole community of faith if we are to avoid misconception and mistake. It is as true of reading the New Testament, as it is of everything else, that reading into the text our own expectations is not a supportable method for understanding what the text is saying. It is though a good method for having the text say what the reader wants it to say!

How much easier it would be if God had dictated the New Testament directly to the prophets and evangelists, because then we could read it literally. In fact we would have to read it literally, because each word, God having spoken it directly, would need to be revered in the very form in which we have it. Doubting or questioning the words would be heretical, and simply taking the words themselves for what they literally say would be the right and proper way to read the New Testament.

Critical analysis would be unnecessary, as we would not need to take a text apart, apply scientific standards to it, examine it as scholars have done and continue to do, trying to better determine exactly when it was written, under what circumstances, and precisely what the author was attempting to say. None of those things would be important if what we had was God's undoubted personal composition. Ah, but since the Bible is not a direct dictation of God, we do need critical study, which I hope will come clear as we continue.

What was clear to the community, from the very beginning of what was to become the Christian faith, was the certainty that the Holy Spirit moved among them. The Spirit's presence was often comforting and consoling, and then sometimes confronting. That is, the spirit was a wind of hope in difficult times, and a forceful gale in more confident times when it challenged, even demanded, a change in life style or attitude. That was the original experience of the presence of the Holy Spirit within the community and remains so for the community of faith today. The New Testament is a living document through which, as the Spirit guides and enables us, we come to know the will and purposes of God for the community of faith in **our** day and time. That, of course, is the crucial concern; what is the New Testament saying to me?

Chapter Five

Early Communities

In his second book, The Acts of the Apostles, Luke describes the early believers as a homogeneous community in which everything was shared, and all held the same views and understanding. This was far from the real situation, for the early community was as diverse in views and understanding as the church is today. The first believers were Jews in Jerusalem and Galilee who had known Jesus and followed him during his ministry. The prime group of his followers, called the disciples or the twelve or the apostles, were all from the area of Galilee, except Judas Iscariot who was a Judean. As Luke relates the story of the Ethiopian eunuch who had come to Jerusalem to worship and was returning home reading the book of Isaiah in his chariot, Phillip's conversion of the man is an example of how quickly the faith had spread out from those two areas into many parts of the empire. (Acts 8: 26) This rapid expansion, taking place not always with adequate instruction in the faith, resulted in conflicting views within the community regarding who Jesus was, what his ministry meant, and how the Resurrection itself was to be understood. It soon became clear that some system, some means of determining the true faith, was required.

While the first and earliest groups of believers were Jews, a lesser number of Gentiles living in Palestine were also part of the community, and it was among those early Jewish members that the first major difficulty arose. While the influence of Judaism upon the early church probably cannot be overstated, Judaism in that early community was not the

Old Testament faith of their fathers. As Christians today read the Hebrew Scripture, the Old Testament, in spite of the continued apostasy of the people, and the warnings and dire predictions of doom by the prophets, what shines out is the relationship between God and his people. God had established a covenant relationship with the people of Israel in which his promise of love and compassion was strong and fearless.

After the return from Babylonian exile, the God of the prophets who walked with his people, looked over them, cared for them, and knew and loved each person intimately drastically changed. The religious leaders developed differing and strongly held views of God's will and demands. While the Scribes, the Pharisees, and the Sadducees were given a bum rap by the New Testament authors; to some extent; they did deserve it. At the time of Jesus the covenant between God and the Jewish people was on the way to being a carefully spelled out system of teachings and oral commentary, which regulated nearly every aspect of life from the length of holy garments to whether or not one could light a fire on the Sabbath. While simplistic to put it this way, it often appeared that the religious leaders were teaching that God cared less about the people themselves, than he did about whether or not they followed the exact letter of the law!

The Gospels contain many examples of how Jesus called this understanding of the Law a distorted view and rebelled against it. Jesus' criticism echoed among many Palestinian Jews, who were equally unhappy with the rigidity of the developing interpretation of the law and sought spiritual understanding in places other than the Hebrew Scriptures. Some of them were attracted to Christianity, some to secular views, some to political rebellion. Some, more orthodox in their belief, agreed with the Jewish leaders that the growing Christianity was a threat or enemy that had to be stopped. The relationship between those Jews who were followers of Jesus and those who were not was difficult from the start.

In the beginning Rome, many Jews, and Christians themselves considered their faith to be a viewpoint or sect within Judaism. This was never entirely accurate; and it quickly began to tear apart when some

Jewish believers insisted that the growing and expanding faith must remain attached to Judaism; because God's promise, though fulfilled in Jesus, was still only for God's chosen people and did not include the Gentiles. This view was neither in accord with the true understanding of Judaism, nor with the Gospel, but it was a strident voice nonetheless. It was also a voice too late. Too many Gentiles were actively involved in the community for this opinion to prevail, and it resulted in a huge disagreement--Gentiles on one side; Jews on another; and many from both sides somewhat in the middle. The tension in this was too brittle to endure, and it soon fractured due to the majority of Jews in Palestine who were not followers of Jesus. While at first they had been tolerant of the Jesus movement, they gradually came to see it as a Jewish heresy. Predictably, this led to persecution of those Jews who followed Jesus by those who did not. Then, as the Jews who followed Jesus retaliated, verbally and angrily, the gulf between the Christian community and the Jewish community widened into a great divide.

This divide was to become an abyss when Hellenistic Jews came into the community. Hellenistic Jews were Jews who had long lived in various parts of the empire, maintained their Jewish allegiance, but were deeply involved in Greek culture and philosophy. The Old Testament was still their Scripture, but rather than reading from the Hebrew, they used a Greek translation, a version called the Septuagint. In essential ways they were as much Greek as they were Jewish, and understood their faith in ways far more congenial to the Greek culture in which they lived, than it was to the traditions and heritage of the Jewish culture in Palestine. Also, more secular than religious, closer to Platonic philosophy than Hebrew theology, Hellenistic Jews were very amenable to the new Christian ideas; and many did join the community. Unbeknownst at the time, this was to bring a new source of theological difficulty for the Christian community in the years to come. Many of the new converts had previously been devotees of a variety of secular views and pagan mystery religions. They brought these ideas with them, and soon divergent views and widely differing theological understandings were literally boiling in the early church.

Far from Luke's ideal of a community of like-minded believers, it was a cauldron of intoxicating possibility as to how the faith should be understood, what could or should be believed, and what must not in any sense be accepted. As this cauldron continued to boil, what might possibly have been worked out was hijacked by the real elephant in the room--Gnosticism. Gnosticism was a widespread philosophy in the Greek-Roman, or Hellenistic, world and was the most significant danger to be imported into the community, as many of the new believers brought gnostic understanding with them. The community did not immediately reject it, for it had a reasonableness and sophistication which was attractive, at least on the surface.

In a general sense, the goal and intention of Gnosticism was a grand synergism of all religions. It melded together Greek philosophy, paganism, Babylonian and Asian myths, Indian, Persian and Jewish religions, and then for a bit of leaven, mixed in the teachings of Jesus. To be sure it was a zesty potpourri, and for the bored and disillusioned world of the first two centuries, a most appetizing dish. A dish that was hard to pass up when the entire world around you offered only a messy porridge of contention and division and constant argument!

Just imagine the pull of the possibility of one grand understanding of God which left out no one and included everyone! All religions! All views! It sounded like the perfect solution to the problems and differences which plagued the community, and the urge of many was to go for it! Had they done that, had they successfully brought the elephant Gnosticism into the community, it would have proven to be a Trojan elephant. The danger hidden within it was that, while the essential message of Christianity was salvation by the grace of God in Christ Jesus, the Gnostics taught that salvation came through "gnosis," a supernatural knowledge others did not have. "Gnosis" imparted the true understanding of God and divine things, but only to those to whom God gave this enlightenment. For some believers this was easily confused with the Holy Spirit, with Jesus' exhortation to Nicodemus that he must be "born again" and with Mark and John's Gospels, which maintained that one could not believe in Jesus unless the Holy Spirit gave that ability. (John 3:1-9) Maybe confusing to some, the differences between the two views were nonetheless huge and impossible. In Gnosticism, there was no need for the community of faith, no need for Jesus, no need for the church organization, no need for the New Testament. It was "God and I are walking together, and we need nothing else." In our 21st century many are again asserting this view, saying that they are "spiritual" but have no need for the community of faith. That is very good Gnosticism. Obviously, for the early community Gnosticism was a wide open door to trouble, just as it is for those who espouse that point of view today.

Gnosticism asserted that the death of Jesus was unnecessary, and Jesus' resurrection irrelevant; because salvation did not require atonement or sacrifice or forgiveness, but simply being enlightened in your understanding. This enlightened understanding had nothing to do with Jesus; it came directly from God in a kind of spiritual ecstasy. Jesus was superfluous and his death simply one of those bad things that happen to good people. The growing popularity of this point of view in our 21st century is good illustration of how attractive it was for some in the early community as well. But this was an impossible position for the community of Jesus' followers. Neither the twelve (11 after Judas), or any of those who had been part of Jesus ministry, could accept this distortion of the faith! For all who had witnessed Jesus' resurrection, although they were still in the process of being led by the Spirit into the full meaning of the resurrection, knew it was neither unnecessary nor unimportant! It was the greatest miracle, the most impossible act of God imaginable; and it changed everything in the world!

To use a boxing metaphor, while the right hook of the gnostic threat--the claim that Jesus was neither necessary nor important to salvation--was easily knocked out by the church; the left uppercut, the second aspect of the Gnostic view, "Dualism," was not as easily dealt with. Dualism had a strong resemblance to Platonic philosophy, which was deeply embedded in the Greek-Roman intellectual worldview of that time. Dualism maintained that the realm of the spiritual was good, but the realm of the flesh was bad. Since God is Spirit, God is above material things and would never have created the material world of the flesh. The material world, the realm of the flesh-- carnal, corrupt, filled with temptations--is ruled by the powers of evil, and is in perpetual war with the spiritual world, ruled by God. Attractive to some, repulsive to others, this caused a great deal of understandable confusion in the community. The four Gospels show a continuous battle between Jesus and the powers of evil, and many did not see a difference between that and what dualism was saying.

The faith of the church was still in process of becoming and was vulnerable to the influence of many philosophical and theological ideas. For example, while it was not present in the beginning of the church because it required a literal understanding of the Old Testament with which not everyone agreed, the doctrine of "original sin" came to have a central role in what was to be the orthodox faith. Orthodoxy put its hand firmly into that of literal interpretation; and Adam and Eve became historical persons, who transmitted their sin through sexual intercourse, from themselves to every human born thereafter. Thus, in the orthodox position, everyone was born with "original sin." It came with birth. The fact that lust and desire are within every person was thought to prove the truth of this doctrine.

Not everyone agreed; nonetheless what had been the majority view in the early community, that God's creation, in all of its parts and aspects had been created good, gradually became the minority view as orthodoxy came into its own. The answer to carnality became spirituality, and soon there was a near stampede to be more spiritual and less material. Holy men and women renounced all material possessions. Those who had been gourmets lived on pods and fruit, and those who sought the strongest spirituality of all--the ascetics, the desert monks, the extreme holy men and women--buried themselves up to their head, or perched in trees, or lived in caves. They pummeled themselves, forbid the desires of the flesh, and mortified their body, all to increase their spirituality.

This was too much for most, so an even larger number pursued a form of spirituality less rigorous, which proved also to be longer lived. These were the mystics and those who were to become the cloistered monks and nuns. Cutting themselves off from the carnal lures of society, they sought a closer relationship with God through denial of material pleasures and cultivation of higher spiritual pursuits. Somewhat popular in limited areas of the church, but never achieving wide acceptance, this approach soon went underground, to reassert itself in the monasticism of the middle Ages. A stepchild of dualism, monasticism was inherently gnostic and non-Christian. It remains in the church today but in a far more "purified' approach, which seeks to be of service to the community rather than to withdraw from it. Cloistered monks and nuns and brothers remain connected to the community as they pray for us all and we are thankful for them. What remains from the gnostic-dualistic battle of the early centuries for those of us, who are not cloistered, is that nagging feeling that we "ought to be" more spiritual and less materialistic than we are. For good or ill, it is a seductive remnant of a view which never totally died out.

Chapter Six

Crucial Importance of the Resurrection

The New Testament is a product of the many experiences of God's people, in differing situations, over generations, during which cultural, social and political views changed dramatically. In addition, the early church was a collection of communities, distant from each other, with limited communication, making it inevitable that within the tradition simple nuances, and sometimes substantial differences of understanding, would develop. A careful reading of the Gospels shows some of these contradictions and opposing views, and shows as well the effort of the Gospel writers to address them.

During Jesus' ministry there was little need for a written record since Jesus was with them. After his resurrection, the disciples were busy; the church was literally exploding and the immediate need was to preach the good news of the resurrection. Then, as the church continued to grow beyond the ability of the eyewitnesses to be personally involved, the desire for a written record of Jesus and his teachings became an irresistible need. The Gospels were written to tell the story of Jesus and serve the needs of the church as it moved into the world. The early church treated the written word as a MEANS to aid preaching and evangelism. That is a fact of critical importance, and we will see how that fact help give shape to the gospels.

The Ministry of Jesus covers the period 27-30 or perhaps 30–33. Dating is somewhat problematic, and while generally thought to have taken place between 30 -33, it is also possible the crucifixion could have been as late as 35 or 36. Whatever the exact date, the years following the resurrection of Jesus are the period of Oral Tradition, which covers the time between the resurrection and the writing of the first Gospel, Mark, written between 45 and 50. For perhaps twenty years the stories about Jesus, what he said, what he did, was shared in the church by the disciples and other followers who spoke out boldly what they had seen. In the telling and retelling the parables, the stories, the words and deeds of Jesus stayed alive and fresh in the community.

Yet, as the years moved on, it is almost certain some change or adaptation of those stories took place. Simply consider how it is to look back from age 50 to something that happened at age 20 or 30; we no longer see with the life experience of a 20 or 30 year old, but with that of a 50 year old. Our recollection is somewhat imprecise and likely colored by the insight and wisdom of age 50, which we did not possess at that earlier age! Even more important, what the community knew about what Jesus said and did during his actual time with them, was dramatically changed by the fact of the resurrection. Also the community itself had changed in many significant ways.

The hundred-year span during which the Gospels and the early church came into existence was a very fluid and intoxicating time of rapid growth. Immediately following Jesus' ministry the oral tradition was collected and written down. Paul wrote his letters between the years 50 and his death about the year 66. Mark wrote between the years 45-50, and quite possibly John at nearly the same time. Then over the next 15-20 years Matthew and Luke wrote their Gospels. During the following years, roughly 70-125, the church became established in many parts of the empire. With establishment often comes a settling in, a damping down of enthusiasm, a reconsideration of possible excess, and a mellowing of the message. This is what happened to the early Christian community and is the crux of many of the interpretation problems which beset us today.

We want the New Testament to be consistent, always saying the same thing. Instead it offers us many differing insights, born of many different experiences of God's presence in the lives of the writers. We discover in the New Testament contradictions, opposing viewpoints, and, to our dismay, often nothing about specific concerns we may bring from our lives, our time and place. Perhaps this is because they were not concerns of that day; but the most likely reason is that the New Testament is concerned about one thing, one glorious and wondrous intention to the whole of it. There is one strong insistent theme beating through every chapter--the story of God's love for all God's creation. The children's song gets right to the heart of it, "Jesus loves me this I know, for the Bible tells me so." We are the beloved children of God. That is the point of it, the essence of it, from the first to the last page. In fact the whole Bible is a love story.

As that story was told, as the writers of Scripture wrote down the accounts of what God had done and was doing in their community, different writers experienced things in different ways, used different sources for their gospel, and addressed different times and places within the community. This not only resulted in differing accounts of the events, but also in different interpretations of what those events meant. Even in the oral traditions, there was what we could call different "theologies," different viewpoints of how God was at work in the world and within the community of faith. The community had many experiences of God, not always understood in the same way. Neither are they today! In the following chapters, we will look carefully at the Gospels of Mark, Matthew, Luke, and John, highlighting some of the similarities and differences we find in the four accounts.

Part Two

A look at the Gospels and Paul

Chapter Seven

Gospel of Mark

Mark was the first gospel written. His principle source was St. Peter, a celebrity source to be sure, and thus Mark's Gospel had high authority in the early community. Almost certainly, Mark also had other sources, but we can only speculate on who or what they may have been. Paul could have been a source, and possibly Mark had personal knowledge as well if he had been involved in the ministry of Jesus. Tradition says Mark was the son of Mary, one of the women who followed Jesus and may have been the young man who fled in the garden of Gethsemane leaving his robe behind. An intriguing possibility but we cannot say for sure.

However, the style of writing, the vivid way in which eyewitness descriptions are given, does suggest that Mark may indeed have been seeing the events himself. The dates of all the Gospels are somewhat tentative; however it is generally agreed Mark wrote within 20 years after Jesus' resurrection. Enough time for a whole generation of oral tradition to have accumulated, Mark tapped into these oral stories, the remembrances of Peter, and perhaps his own and his mother's memories as well.

Mark has a special purpose in writing his Gospel, and he states it clearly in the first verse "... the beginning of the Gospel about Jesus Christ, the Son of God. " (Mark 1:1) The word he uses for Good News, *"euaggelion,"* is the Greek word for news of a victory in battle, a word Mark chose deliberately because the whole thrust of his Gospel is to show that Jesus "won the battle" over Satan, and thus over Sin. That is Mark's goal, and as his Gospel moves along in achieving this, Mark presents a carefully crafted story of Jesus' ministry in a series of encounters, healings and other occurrences, all with the single goal of showing Jesus to be the Son of God.

Perhaps the best comparison for Mark's Gospel would be with an historical novel. Mark has all the elements: character development, an engrossing plot, unexpected twists and a cliffhanger ending. The gospel is truly a thrilling narrative of suspense, and the reader cannot but be caught up in the story-- the plot, the characters, and then that suspenseful ending. As the many people come to Jesus seeking help, Mark tells us that while Jesus always dealt with their presented problem, he then offered them more than they knew they needed or expected to receive, and then gave an invitation to follow him. This is essential to Mark who is saying to his readers that every time we meet Jesus, in whatever way he comes to us, it is a time of decision; in our every experience of Jesus, we make a decision for him or against him. All who are followers of Jesus are with him in a battle against evil, and in that battle, our decisions to follow Jesus or reject him will either deepen our faith or harden our heart. Mark presents this assertion brilliantly in story after story. When someone accepts the invitation and becomes a disciple, Mark shows that discipleship brings both challenges and abundant blessings. For those who refuse to follow Jesus, there are no dire consequences in their life, as we might expect, but rather a great sadness within Jesus.

Each of the four Gospels has a preface. Mark's is the shortest and opens with an account of John the Baptist. This is deliberate, for Mark is setting Jesus' ministry within the context of the Old Testament, which was Scripture for that early community of Christians, and it was important to show that Jesus was in accord with the prophecies of Scripture regarding the Messiah. However Mark begins with John the Baptist for another even more powerful reason; John comes, and people from "the whole country side" are there to hear him. A dramatic way for Mark to say that in John everything is exploding, a new world is dawning, and a new beginning will soon be upon us in Jesus! (1:5)

Mark does not have any nativity stories. Perhaps Mark did not include the birth stories because for the early community of believers there was little interest in them. The resurrection proved Jesus was God's son and it wasn't important to them exactly how this was true, or when it became true; they knew it **was** true! They had no doubt, because they experienced the risen Jesus and that proved who he was. The important thing therefore was to proclaim what God had done, not write a biography. Jesus' birth was not as important as proclaiming the resurrection. Little else mattered than to literally run to tell the world of this incredible act of God.

Jesus WAS the Son of God, they knew that, and their only concern was to proclaim it. Nothing else mattered. They expected the imminent return of Jesus, so they got right to doing as Jesus told them, proclaiming the good news to all people. Everything else paled before the one thing of supreme importance that in Jesus we are all embraced in a wondrous new relationship as the sons and daughters of God.

The return of Jesus did not happen as soon as they had expected however, and the church settled in for a longer wait. In the waiting, the priority of the early community gave way to the new needs of worship, liturgy, and the developing church year and holy days, all of which demanded a more detailed accounting of when, how, in what way Jesus became the Son of God. Matthew and Luke were soon to fulfill this need. Although Mark does not include birth stories, Jesus' baptism is of utmost importance to him. It is the beginning of Jesus' ministry, and the manner in which it takes place is crucial to the whole thrust of Mark's Gospel. We will look deeper into that in the next chapter.

Chapter Eight

Baptism of Jesus as insight to Mark

When we consider what Mark says about Jesus' baptism, we see immediately how different Mark's account is from the same account in the other Gospels. In Verses 9-11 Marks account is much like John's and very unlike Matthew and Luke.

In Mark's account of the baptism he says Jesus saw the heavens open, the Spirit descending upon him like a dove, and heard a voice saying, "You are my beloved Son with whom I am well pleased." Mark presents the story as God's validation of Jesus, given to him alone, no one else able to see the dove or hear the voice. This is critical to Mark because, if they had heard and seen, it would have been overpowering evidence requiring them to accept Jesus as God's Son and believe in him. How could they not? However, throughout his Gospel Mark repeatedly makes the point that it is never clear that Jesus is either who he says he is or whom his words and deeds might show him to be. The encounter is always ambiguous and happens in such a way that it is a time of decision whether to believe or not. There is no objective evidence which convinces beyond doubt. There is always need for trust and faith. Interesting, I think, that this same ambiguity and lack of proof' is present also in John's Gospel. Mark's account of Jesus' baptism shows this clearly, for the voice of God affirms that Jesus is God's son, but the crowd hears nothing, it is completely a personal experience of Jesus.

That raises a question. If only Jesus heard the voice, how did Mark know what was said? Mark knew his Hebrew Scripture and realized that two passages applied to Jesus baptism: Psalm 2:7 "The Lord said to me 'Today you are my son, today I have begotten you." and Isaiah 42.1 "This is my servant I have put my spirit upon him." Since only Jesus heard the words, Mark could not personally have known what God said to Jesus but was certain in some way God would have validated Jesus in the act of his baptism. That is very much exactly what the sacrament of baptism does for us--validate us as a child of God. So Mark applies the word of God given to the community in the Hebrew Scriptures to relate what God surely would have said to Jesus, for it is what God says to all who are baptized in His name. In this we see the manner in which the whole community wrote the New Testament; the Jewish and the soon to be Christian communities shared the presence of God within their fellowships of faith. The word of God to the Jews was not out of date in Jesus, but fulfilled and given new meaning. Both Jews and Christians are part of the family of God in which the Holy Spirit is at work.

Mark's statement following Jesus' baptism is crucial to understanding his Gospel. He tells us, "Immediately the Spirit drove Jesus into the wilderness. He was in the wilderness forty days, tempted by Satan; and he was with the wild beasts; and the angels waited upon him. (1:12). That's Mark's whole temptation account!   Matthew and Luke take ten times as long to tell of the event and put in all that detail about Jesus enduring three episodes of successive temptation. John does not record this event at all, and in this, we see how each author chose what he wanted to include in his Gospel, and left out what he did not want to include. Mark wants to show that Immediately after Jesus' baptism and the declaration to him that he is the beloved of God the Spirit drives Jesus into the wilderness. This is a very critical extremely important assertion for Mark, because in Jesus God begins the war against the powers of evil. God sends his own son to battle with the devil, the same foe we must face. Jesus must face temptation as we too must face it. This is a major point for Mark, that Jesus fights our battle against sin and the power of evil.

Mark makes it clear from the very beginning that Jesus' ministry will not lead to glory, but to death and abandonment. Jesus life and death is a total identification with the life of human beings, including all the temptations, trials and dangers that assault us. In our place, and on our behalf, Jesus does battle with evil and rejection, ridicule and suffering; and like us, his life too will end in death. Mark is clear; Jesus is fully human, totally like us in every way. His whole ministry is part of God's plan to conquer sin and death on our behalf; so when, like every human person, Jesus is led into temptation, he is led there by the Spirit. Mark is saying it is God's will that Jesus endure all that we endure, experience all that we experience. Jesus however does not give in to temptation as we do, and withstanding the temptation, he prevails over sin, and in prevailing, redeems the fallen creation and restores us to fellowship with God.

What Mark is also telling us in this account, which he is at pains to say throughout his Gospel, is that whoever accepts the call to follow Jesus must enter into the same battle with Satan and temptation that Jesus did. It is a battle which will last throughout our lives, never letting up. But one we do not fight alone for Jesus is with us; and the amazing, wondrous peace and love of God will be there to support us. This is the reason Mark mentions that the angels supported Jesus in the wilderness. Angels, a metaphor for the strength and presence of God, were there for Jesus and will be there for us as well.

It is the heart of Mark's incredibly realistic Gospel to tell us that, as followers of Jesus, not only will we experience the temptation in the wilderness, but in some manner our own experience of Gethsemane and Golgotha as well. As Jesus is in solidarity with us, so also we must be in solidarity with him in the battle against sin and death. Mark is clear that there will be times in our faith when we want to give up, times when we are stressed to our limit and tempted to despair. Then for us, as for Jesus in his temptation, the strength and peace of God, and the ministry of the angels, will be there for us too. No matter what comes, those threatening wild animals that did not harm Jesus will not harm us either. "Wild animals" are Mark's metaphor for all the ills and fears that would claim us, but which for all their noise and fearfulness have no power over us when we are in Jesus, just as they had no power over him. That is what Mark is saying.

Then, as a way of reassuring us, telling us not to be overwhelmed by the task before us, Mark says that Jesus brings an end to the old age and the beginning of a new age. Jesus brings a new covenant, one in which God is present and at work in his church, the body of Christ, just as he was present and at work among the people of God in the Old Testament. He will lead us through whatever befalls into his kingdom. Beautiful metaphors abound, and what powerful words they were for the young emerging church to hear!   What great words for us as well!

Chapter Nine

Mark...continued

As Mark's Gospel narrates the story of Jesus' ministry it does so from the viewpoint of Mark himself, not as the other Gospels which do so from the viewpoint of the bystanders, the disciples, or an unnamed commentator. This method is unique to the Gospel of Mark.

Although not unique to Mark, for he shares the insight with John's Gospel, Mark stresses that the kingdom of God is with us in Jesus. Note the present tense: the kingdom **is here.** Mark wants it clear the kingdom is not only coming someday, in a thousand years or so, but that it came among us in Jesus, and it comes for each of us individually in every encounter we have with Jesus. And it is in that very moment of encounter that, depending upon the choice we make, it is decided whether we will or will not be in the kingdom. If we accept the call of Jesus to follow him, in that decision we are brought into the kingdom immediately. In that moment we become a disciple of Jesus. Paul had the same understanding: when we are "in Christ," he said, we are also in God and thus we are in the kingdom. We see how this works when Jesus calls the first disciples and they drop everything and follow him. That's how it must be. No second thoughts....just do it, because if we do not respond the first time, it becomes easier not to respond the second time, and soon we no longer care to respond at all!

This concept of the call of Jesus through the Holy Spirit and our response to it is central and crucial to Mark. Actually, this is so in all the Gospels, but Mark makes it especially clear that, while the miracles and healings and preaching of Jesus were obvious out in the open events, they meant nothing, made no sense, to those who would not allow the Holy Spirit to open their eyes. They remained, in a sense, blind, for without the agency of the Spirit they might see but they didn't see! They may have heard but they didn't hear. This is a basic assertion in Mark's Gospel, and it comes directly from Jesus. In all the incidents recorded in his Gospel, in meeting Jesus the person is brought to a decision point in which he or she either believes or does not believe.

But then is now; for Mark goes on to say that, for each of us, in the experience to which the Holy Spirit leads us in our lives today, it is equally as personal and subjective a decision for or against Jesus as it was for those who saw, heard and met Jesus in the flesh. Mark would say those who lived at that time have no advantage over those who lived later because the same experience is true for every believer; there is always a confronting and a decision. And as it was for the original hearers of Jesus, when we do come to faith, when we do choose to follow Jesus, it is ultimately not so much our decision as the work of the Holy Spirit. Once again, Then is Now!

Of all the gospels, Mark perhaps best represents the faith of the early community. The overall theme of Mark is Jesus, the Son of God vs. the powers of evil, i.e., the Devil or Satan; and the Holy Spirit vs Unclean Spirits. The battle rages, life is a constant struggle between life and death. But, whether we understand it fully or not, it is also a battle between a life within a community of faith and a life on our own, lived in segregation and loneliness. It is a choice, and it cannot be evaded.

To underscore that theme, Mark shows us that the cosmic battle is ushered in by Jesus' baptism and temptation, an event blessed by God in which history is redeemed from its dead-end journey and set off on a new course. In Jesus God enters human life. It is a watershed moment, and history from then forward becomes a battle to the death between God and Evil, and between Evil and all who follow Jesus. We cannot be merely spectators to this battle. There can be no neutrality, and we are required to choose which side we are on. Faced with this stark reality, it is of great comfort for sinners like us that the disciples do not come across as heroes in Mark! They misunderstand or do not understand... continually. They repeatedly do the wrong thing, and in those times when they do not follow Jesus, their minds are hardened, their understanding is further darkened, their faith falters, and they become confused rather than certain. Mark says this is always the case with Satan who blinds us to the truth, and we cannot see it as long as we are in the company of evil.

Mark shows us how the struggle of Jesus began in the temptation in the wilderness and continued in all the confrontations with demons, including the debates with the religious authorities, who are seen to be on evil's side. Even the disciples become allies of Satan at those times when they push aside the truth that discipleship requires us not only to join in the battle but to accept the suffering that may come from that battle. Jesus predicts the cross for himself; they deny any such requirement, either for him or themselves and thereby show they are of the world, not of the Spirit. They must repent and turn again to the battle. We, as they, must be engaged in the fight; for Mark makes it extremely clear the coming of Jesus is the coming of the Kingdom of God in a decisive way, that in him all history is moving toward the time of consummation. Jesus' resurrection was not only a dramatic vindication of the Gospel; it was the decisive defeat of the powers of evil, a triumph over the power of death, the devil and sin. In Jesus' resurrection the reign of God begins.

I finish the section on Mark with what may be a somewhat surprising assertion. In Mark's view we are saved not by what Jesus did, as we have so often heard, but we are saved by our <u>participation</u> in what Jesus did. It is by our entering the struggle together with him, fighting against doubt, evil and sin in our own lives that we become one with the Lord. Jesus took his cross to Golgotha; we are to pick up ours and carry it where God sends us as faithful disciples. Our participation does not earn us our salvation, that is a gift of God's grace; but lack of participation in the battle against evil, trying to sit on the fence or on the sidelines, puts our fate in great jeopardy because every time we do not choose to follow Jesus, our heart becomes hardened and less willing to do so next time. When we

are faithful, every time we choose to follow Jesus, our faith is strengthened, and we continue the battle, knowing that in Jesus we have certainty
of victory. Mark insists it is in the moment of our decision for Jesus that
we are brought into the kingdom of God. So he says to us and all who
read him, in effect, "Now is the hour of your redemption."

You may have noticed that nothing has been said about the ending
of Mark's gospel and his account of the resurrection, which continue to
be very controversial in the church. We will deal with that and with all the
resurrection accounts in later chapters.

Chapter Ten

Gospel of Matthew

Mark was incredibly popular, copied and used throughout the church. But a generation later the church developed a thirst for more information about Jesus. When was he born? What else happened in addition to what Mark wrote? And why did Mark not include the resurrection appearances of Jesus? For this later generation of believers Mark's gospel was inadequate. In the years following Mark's publication many concerns and interests in the church changed. There was so much that Mark had not included and a more detailed gospel was needed. Matthew stepped up and became the second gospel written.

Matthew makes extensive use of Mark's Gospel; such extensive use Matthew must have had a copy of Mark on the table before him. 11/12ths of Mark is included in Matthew! And it is an exact copy of Mark, although rearranged to fit into Matthew's design for his Gospel. Why would Matthew copy Mark? The most generally accepted explanation is that because Peter, who is the authority behind Mark's gospel, was so highly revered in the early community that Matthew did not want to appear to be trying to supersede him. This is a reasonable hypothesis, for we know the community was conservative and reverent regarding holy texts; and since Mark was regarded as Peter's memoirs, and perhaps Mark's as well, the Gospel had to be treated with utmost respect. Whether that is the reason or not, the 11/12ths of Mark that he copied makes up 1/3 of Matthew's Gospel.

Matthew had his own sources for the other 2/3 of his Gospel but we are not sure what these other sources may have been. Aristotle supposedly said that nature abhors a vacuum. Bible scholars do as well; and not knowing Matthew's sources, scholars proposed the existence of a document named "Q", from the Greek word Quelle, which means "source." This theory suggests "Q" was an eye witness account, perhaps a form of diary, written in Aramaic, recording the things Jesus said and did throughout his ministry. Bishop Papias of Hierapolis (100–140) is responsible for this idea; for he claimed Matthew had collected the sayings of Jesus in the Hebrew language. This claim fueled the speculation that it was "Q" and a source for the Gospel of Matthew and perhaps Luke, in part, as well. While the claim of Papias is not to be lightly treated "Q" does not exist as a document, and if it was an early account of Jesus' ministry, considering the high respect in which such documents were regarded in the early community, it is very unlikely it would have been allowed to be lost. It would have been far too valuable. So if it existed, it should still exist! Unless, as one theory maintains, Matthew incorporated all of it into his Gospel, so there was no need to preserve it as a stand-alone document. Well, hmm, maybe. Another possibility, which is just beginning to receive more detailed examination, is that a document called the "Gospel of Thomas," might be that lost or elusive "Q"! (We will look at this later.)

There is at least one more possibility; Matthew's Gospel contains many sayings of Jesus and incidents in Jesus' ministry which are not included in the other Gospels. It could be, as a strong tradition in the early church maintains, that the author was the disciple Matthew; and if so then his "other source" was himself! The church father Clement, Bishop of Rome during the years 88 to perhaps 100, quoted Matthew in sermons and writings. Unfortunately Clement did not say who the author was, and the usual evidence used to determine authorship, based upon those textual tools we discussed previously, is inconclusive; that is, maybe the disciple Matthew, or maybe not.

So, we are not sure who wrote Matthew; and even when he wrote his Gospel is somewhat contentious. It had to have been written after Mark, and a date soon after Mark is suggested by the fact that Matthew's intended audience was the Jewish and Jewish-Christian community, which composed the majority of the early believers. If the disciple Matthew did write the Gospel, this too indicates a date between 55 and 60+.

The authorship of Matthew is not clear, but the purpose of the Gospel is very clear; Matthew's intended readers were the Jews in the early community. The Jewish members had a particular concern as to whether or not Jesus was the Messiah long promised in their Scripture and history. Matthew writes to address this concern; to convince those who were reluctant to accept Jesus as Messiah, and to reassure those who had accepted him that indeed Jesus is the long awaited Messiah. The way in which Matthew sets about his task is very creative and quite clever.

The chapters and verses of the New Testament as we have them today were somewhat arbitrarily determined by the Archbishop Stephen Langton in the 13th century. Prior to Langton, chapter and verse divisions did not exist in the original manuscripts, and Matthew's Gospel, like all New Testament documents, did not have divisions into chapters or verses, but was one continuous document. It was Matthew's originality to arrange his Gospel into a prologue, followed by 5 sections and an epilog. Each section, ended with the phrase, "And it came to pass when Jesus had finished this saying...." Then the next section begins.

Those five sections, in our present day ordering of the Gospel are:

Prologue	Chapters	1 and 2
Book 1	Chapters	3 -7
Book 2	Chapters	8-10
Book 3	Chapters	11-13
Book 4	Chapters	14-18
Book 5	Chapters	19-25
Epilog	Chapters	26-28

The clever intention in this arrangement is to somewhat replicate the Torah, the first five books of the Old Testament, which are especially sacred to the Jewish faith. Matthew is saying the Gospel of Jesus is the new Torah! Matthew ties Jesus tightly to the Hebrew Scripture and shows again and again that what Jesus said and did was in accordance with what the Hebrew Scripture said about the Messiah, and thus Jesus "fulfilled the Scriptures."

Perhaps because of his overall thrust to show that Jesus was the Messiah sent by God, Matthew downplays the humanity of Jesus and emphasizes his relationship to God. In Matthew's view, since the resurrection of Jesus proved that he was God's son, it seemed only logical that his relationship with God would have been obvious throughout Jesus' ministry. How could he keep that hidden?

So when Matthew copies Mark, he removes those situations in which Mark shows the human limitations of Jesus. For example, Mark says of Jesus, "And he could do no deed of power there, except that he laid his hands on a few sick people and cured them."(6:5) Matthew thought that could never be true for Jesus so he removes it. And when in Mark Jesus says to a young man, "Why do you call me good?" Matthew, who knew that Jesus was of course good, changes Mark to read "Why do you ask me about the good?" (Mk 10:18) (Mt 19:17) And Matthew, more in accord with the culture of the time than with Jesus' view, considered it beneath a divine Jesus to stoop to converse with a child, much less hold one, so when Mark tells us Jesus took a little child in his arms (9:28), Matthew simply removes this incident. In a number of places where Mark mistakenly references something in the Hebrew Bible, Matthew, perhaps knowing better, leaves those things out as well. And Matthew makes it clear that it is only his divine nature as the Son of God that gives Jesus the authority to say, "It was said of old ... but I say to you."

It is interesting that Matthew exalts Peter high above the other disciples. Only in his Gospel does Peter walk on water (17: 24) and only in Matthew does Jesus say, "You are Peter. And on this rock I will build my church." (16:18). This exaltation of Peter's role among the disciples is not supported in the other Gospel accounts; Mark (8:27-35) and Luke (9:18-20) have this exact same story, but without Jesus' comment to Peter.

Matthew wanted to convince the Jewish members that Jesus was the Messiah; indeed, more than that alone, Jesus was the Son of God. His goal was achieved. Matthew was successful beyond his expectations, for as the church moved out of Palestine and into the wider world, even as Luke and John took the Gospel total to four, Matthew's Gospel remained the most popular of them. It is still the favorite of many.

Chapter Eleven

Gospel of Luke and the book of Acts

Luke

Finally we can say something with certainty! There is no doubt that the author of Luke, and of Acts, is the Luke whom Paul tells us in Colossians was a physician. (4:14) In his second letter to Timothy (4:11) and his letter to Philemon (1:24) Paul adds that Luke was his companion who traveled with him for a time. While not said, it is certain Luke was a Gentile. This companionship with Paul is another reason to support the earlier dating for Luke which would then make Luke the last gospel written, about the year 63, only 33 years after the crucifixion.

Three strong assumptions give us this date. The first assumption is really closer to being a fact, for it is quite obvious that Luke makes extensive use of Mark, which sets the earliest possible date for Luke's Gospel as being after Mark. The second assumption is that Luke copied some of the sayings and incidents in Matthew into his Gospel, would determine the dating of Luke as being after Matthew. We know Luke wrote the book of Acts after his Gospel. The main character in Acts is Paul, and Acts ends with Paul on his way to Rome. Paul was put to death in Rome around 63-65, yet Acts says nothing about it. If Paul's death had been a past event, Luke would without question have mentioned it, and the fact that Acts does not mention Paul's death is considered reason enough to date both the Gospel of Luke and the book of Acts around 63 or 65, before Paul died.

Another reason for asserting Luke was the last Gospel written in the sequence of gospels is his acknowledgment that he is the last! He says in the first chapter, 1:1 "....*Since many have undertaken to set down an orderly account of the events that have been fulfilled among us, ² just as they were handed on to us by those who from the beginning were eyewitnesses and servants of the word, ³ I too decided, after investigating everything carefully from the very first,*[a] *to write an orderly account for you, most excellent Theophilus, ⁴ so that you may know the truth concerning the things about which you have been instructed.*

We do not know who Theophilus was, though the title "most excellent" indicates he was a high official, perhaps a Roman authority. In the preface to Acts, also dedicated to Theophilus, Luke acknowledges Acts to be the second book in his series.

Luke says "...accounts of the events were handed down to us..." Luke made use of those other accounts. He reproduced 53% of Mark verbatim, exact same words and phrases. He almost surely also had a copy of Matthew before him as well; and even though he often chooses to deviate from Matthew in favor of his own sources, 200 verses in Luke are identical to those in Matthew. However, one-half of Luke is original to him and contains information not in the other Gospels. In the beginning of his Gospel Luke tells us two interesting things; that "others" have written accounts, and that he intends to do a final and most complete version. In at least one sense he accomplished this, for Luke is the longest of the four gospels, and arguably the most complete. By the time Luke wrote, the Gentile membership of the church was growing rapidly; and thanks to the missionary efforts of Paul, the community of faith, which had started with a small group of Jewish converts, had spread widely through the Greek-Roman world. Luke wrote his two books for these Gentile converts, his intention to show that Jesus is the savior not only for the Jews but for the world, all nations and all peoples.

The entire first three chapters of Luke's Gospel contain material not mentioned in the other four. Luke deals with the birth of John the Baptist, the angel visit to Mary, Mary's visit to Elizabeth, the Magnificat, the birth of John, the birth of Jesus, the story of Jesus in the temple as a boy, John the Baptist in the wilderness, and a genealogy of Jesus. We will deal with these stories later when we discuss the birth and infancy narratives of Jesus. The point here is that none of these accounts are mentioned anywhere but in Luke.

Luke tells Theophilus the purpose of his Gospel is to assure Romans and all lovers of God as to the certainty of the things they have heard about Jesus. The probability that Theophilus was a high ranking Roman official is increased by the secondary concern of Luke's Gospel, to show that Jesus was not the political revolutionary he was accused of being when he was crucified. Luke wants to make it clear that Christians, as was Jesus, are upright noble citizens of Rome.

Luke was a second generation Christian, but while he was not an eye witness himself, he had first hand acquaintance with some of those who were eyewitnesses to Jesus' ministry. This fact gives credibility to his non-Mark and non-Matthew material. In Acts, Luke mentions how "we" (Luke, Paul, and maybe others) spent a night with Mnason, an original disciple or follower of Jesus. Mnason, who came from Cyprus, accompanied Paul on his last journey and Paul stayed in his home. (21:16). It is also quite probable, verging on certainty, that since Luke traveled with Paul, he had also met Peter and James the brother of Jesus. Perhaps these are also sources Luke used for his Gospel.

Luke writes highly polished Greek so he was a well-educated person. He is interested in Gentile concerns, but also conversant with the Old Testament. Interestingly, while Luke delights in miracles and supernatural intervention which show the power of Jesus, he develops the idea that Jesus' awareness of himself as the Son of God came to him slowly over a period of time. The incident in the temple at age 12 showed he was thinking along those lines, but still not clearly certain of it. It is that uncertainty which is tested by Satan in Luke's version of the temptation story. We looked extensively at Mark's story of Jesus' temptation; now we need to consider Matthew and Luke as well. Luke and Matthew are identical, except Luke reverses the order of the temptations, suggesting Luke may have copied the story from Matthew.

Recall from our discussion of Matthew that he wrote primarily for the Jewish Christians, to show or prove to them that Jesus did fulfill all the prophecies in the Hebrew Bible. Thus in Matthew's story of the tempta- tion the statements Jesus makes in rebuttal to Satan are quotations from the book of Deuteronomy, "One does not live by bread alone, but by every word that comes from the mouth of the Lord."(8:3) "The Lord your God you shall fear; him you shall serve, and by his name alone you shall swear" (6:13) and "Do not put the Lord your God to the test." (6:16). These quotes are taken from the account of Israel's troubles in the desert, but the fact that Matthew applies them so easily to Jesus shows us how the Hebrew Scripture was the scripture for the early community and was re- garded as God's word to the Christians as well as the Jews.

Luke's temptation account differs from Matthew only in that he rear- ranges the sequence of the temptations and adds an ominous closing statement that the devil "...departed from him until an opportune time." (4:13) Luke may be looking ahead to the attempt of the people of Nazareth to throw Jesus off "a high place" (4:29), but whether that is so or not, some neat things happen in Luke's account of Jesus' temptation. He tells us Jesus endured 40 days of trial including three specific temptations. Two of them are introduced, "If you are God's son," a clear connection to 3:22 where God said to Jesus at his baptism, "You are my son." 40 days is a symbolic term used to indicate a very long time. In this long time Jesus experiences solitude, fasting, and an existential wresting with what hap- pened in his baptism; "What does it mean, what does God want of me?" For Luke, at this point in his ministry Jesus is not yet clear of his mission.

The first temptation (4:4) hits Jesus on two levels. Satan says, "If Moses could feed his people with bread from heaven, then surely you, Jesus, if you are God's son, could do it too!" The second level then con- trasts Jesus' divinity with his humanity; Jesus is hungry, starving, why not take the stones and make bread? The second temptation (4:5) to wealth and material possessions would surely have resonated with Jesus if, as Luke suggests, he is not yet certain of his mission. Jesus has given up his livelihood; and no longer a carpenter, he enters a ministry in which he is dependent upon handouts, supporters and patrons, so it must have been, "tempting"! The third temptation (4:9) to in effect tempt God by throwing himself off the temple roof is perhaps a moment of dramatic decision for Jesus. He dismisses Satan with the words from Deuteronomy 6:16 "Do not put the Lord your God to the test!" It sounds as if it suddenly did become clear to Jesus that he was God's Son. If so, the put-down of Satan has a double meaning, referring to God and to himself! "Do not test God...or me. Enough already, Satan!"

In Luke's account the three temptations are symbolic; that is, they took place in Jesus' inward, imaginative, or psychological experience. Oh yes, they were real, very real, so profoundly real Jesus remembered this experience throughout his ministry and made various, although indirect, references of it to his disciples. Luke's last two temptations are the very ones Jesus was to encounter as his ministry progressed: the temptation of the people when they tried to make Jesus King and "...he departed into a mountain," and then on the cross, when the religious leaders, acting as agents of Satan, say to him ..."If you are the Son of God why don't you come down?" Luke tells us throughout his Gospel that Jesus always responded to suggestions he use his power for himself by saying the kingdom belongs not to him but to God. Thank you, Luke, for reminding us not to be so quick to put Jesus in God's place---the kingdom is God's. God gave it to Jesus, but it was not his as a right.

The devil's temptation to worship him and gain all the kingdoms of the world is replicated again during Jesus' ministry. He was often recruited to join with the powers trying to overthrow Rome. They were called Zealots, and it is probable Judas was one of them, and Jesus' refusal to join may have played a part in Judas' betrayal. The Zealots were popular with many in Israel who hated the Roman occupation. Barabbas was almost certainly a Zealot, which could be why he was chosen to be freed rather than Jesus. Jesus rejected the whole idea that political power, military power, any kind of power in that sense, can achieve the kingdom of God. Maybe it can advance the kingdom of this world; but by comparison, that's a very different and very limited achievement. Luke says Jesus overcomes the temptation to an earthly kingdom, which was exactly what Israel wanted the Messiah to embrace; and when he rejected it, they rejected him, and decided to get rid of him.

The second level to Jesus' third temptation is the most devious and one which comes to all of us as well: the idea that a special call from God would prove itself by signs. Is that not a temptation with which we are all familiar? We want a sign that we are doing what God wants. We want to be sure things are in good shape between us and God. This was to be a constant temptation during Jesus' ministry as repeatedly the people asked him for a sign. Always Jesus would sigh. Twice in Luke's Gospel he said, "No sign shall be given to this generation."(11; 16, 29) To John the Baptist, who asked for a sign, Jesus said with exasperation, "Tell John what you see ..." (7:22)

Over against all three temptations Jesus quotes from Deuteronomy, indicating that God's will has been clear from ancient days and nothing has changed. God's will is to be trusted and obeyed. We must live by faith not by signs and wonders.

Acts

In addition to his Gospel, Luke wrote the book of Acts and, taken together, they give us a picture of the early community of believers about 30 years after the resurrection. The story in Acts goes something like this:

During his ministry the teaching of Jesus was being well received by the people. But, as his following grew, the religious leaders correctly perceived that this new teaching threatened the worldview of Judaism, the structures and ideas which had always been considered to be eternally true. This antagonized the established religious leaders, who for the most part saw Jesus as a threat and reacted from that very existential concern. Since Jesus was a threat, they became defensive and protective of the status quo.

The Gospels also tell us that early in Jesus' ministry the religious authorities were close-minded regarding both the man and his message and began to collect evidence against him. Without question Jesus was often short with them, pointed and antagonistic in his comments, calling them "Vipers, whitewashed tombstones, devils." Jesus clearly realized his ministry was a watershed break with the old ways, an understanding he expressed very dramatically when he said, "Whoever does not leave father and mother behind to follow me is not worthy of me." (Matthew 10:37, Luke 14:26)   In these verses and many others Jesus made clear that in him a totally new understanding of God had broken in upon the world.

The supernatural intervention of which Luke is so fond, as we will see in the birth and resurrection stories, is also prominently present in his book of Acts. We only need to consider a few of them to realize that Luke was enamored of miracles as being a means of proving the power of Jesus remained with the disciples and in the church. All the following are from Acts in which Luke tells us:

1.   The disciples performed miracles

"Now many signs and wonders were done among the people through the apostles. And they were all together in Solomon's Portico (5:12) "A great number of people would also gather from the towns around Jerusalem, bringing the sick and those tormented by unclean spirits, and they were all cured." (5:16)

2.   Paul performed miracles as well.

"And in Lystra there was a man sitting who could not use his feet and had never walked, for he had been crippled from birth. [9] He listened to Paul as he was speaking. And Paul, looking at him intently and seeing that he had faith

to be healed, [10] said in a loud voice, "Stand upright on your feet." And the man[a] sprang up and began to walk. (14:8-10)

"But Saul, also known as Paul, filled with the Holy Spirit, looked intently at him [10] and said—the hand of the Lord is against you, and you will be blind for a while, unable to see the sun." Immediately mist and darkness came over him, and he went about groping for someone to lead him by the hand. ." (13:8-11).

"But Paul, very much annoyed, turned and said to the spirit, "I order you in the name of Jesus Christ to come out of her." And it came out that very hour. (16:16-18)

Luke even outdoes himself when he says, *"God did extraordinary miracles through Paul, [12] so that when the handkerchiefs or aprons that had touched his skin were brought to the sick, their diseases left them, and the evil spirits came out of them."* (19:11-12), Then, in an over-the-top statement, Luke says Paul could even raise the dead: "A young man named Eutychus, who was sitting in the window, began to sink off into a deep sleep while Paul talked still longer. Overcome by sleep, he fell to the ground three floors below and was picked up dead. [10] But Paul went down, and bending over him took him in his arms, and said, "Do not be alarmed, for his life is in him."" (20:9-10)

There are fifteen miracles in the books of Acts, many performed by Paul, but Peter outdoes them all when Acts claims Peter not only raised the dead, (9:36-41) but that his shadow alone was enough to heal the sick (5:15). When Paul and Silas are imprisoned "There was an earthquake, so violent that the foundations of the prison were shaken; and immediately all the doors were opened and everyone's chains were unfastened." (16:25,26) Luke loves miracles, and perhaps the greatest miracle he recounts was his total deification of human nature when he tells us that in the early church community, *"All who believed were together and had all things in common; they would sell their possessions and goods and distribute the proceeds to all, as any had need. Day by day, as they spent much time together in the temple, they broke bread at home and ate their food with glad and generous hearts, praising God and having the good-will of all the people."* (2:45) I will leave the veracity of Luke's miracles to your own decision; but the truth regarding the early community, as we have seen, and will see in more detail later, was something quite other than Luke's description!

The Last of the Gospels to be written, Luke is of extreme importance to the church, both in the earliest days and still for us today. Luke is an "apologia," a book written to show to Theophilus and to the Gentile world that Jesus was, in his person, in himself, God come among us in human life. The other Gospels; in fact all the other writings in the New Testament, were written primarily for the community of the church. Luke however wrote for an audience which, while to be sure was inclusive of the community, was primarily intended for those who were outside the community, to provide the solid facts, the real truth, the meaning and purpose of Jesus' life and ministry. Christians were regarded with suspicion in the Roman world, and a secondary but extremely important purpose in Luke's two books, is to demonstrate that the followers of Jesus were not revolutionaries and did not pose a threat to Rome. In fact Jesus disavowed rebellion against Rome, and advocated obedience to the empire. In the years in which the gospels were being written Israel and Rome entered a tense and untenable situation which ended in the destruction of Jerusalem In the year 70. So Luke's concern writing in the mid 60's was more than reasonable.

Chapter Twelve

Gospel of John

The German scholars of the 19th century decided John was the last Gospel written, roughly dated around 90, almost 60 years after the Resurrection. This opinion was based in large part upon two facts; first, that John is so obviously different in style and approach from the synoptic gospels; Mark, Matthew and Luke, focusing less upon when something happened and more upon what it meant that it happened. That decision largely shaped their second supposition: that the understanding of Jesus' relationship to God, termed "Christology" is so highly developed in John, it could not have been present in the early community but would have required at least two generations of reflection to be achieved. These two conclusions judged John to be of a much later origin and therefore not of the same value to scholars as the synoptic gospels.

All this has all changed in recent times as scholars now suspect John may have been written somewhat contemporaneously with Mark. The argument that the Christology in John represents an understanding too sophisticated for an early composition is easily and rather quickly demolished when we compare John's Christology with a number of Paul's letters, written in the 50's. Paul's Christology is just as "advanced" or "sophisticated" as that in John. While this new view regarding John would have scandalized those German scholars a generation ago, they would surely have changed their opinion, had they been aware of the papyrus discoveries since the 19th century, which have now dated the Gospel of

John to the middle of the first century, a date basically contemporary to, or earlier than, all the other Gospels. We will discuss those papyri in a following chapter.

But, whenever it was written, John indeed is the most carefully and obviously theological of the four gospels; the 19th century German scholars were right about that. Even though John's Gospel has been proven in more recent research to be very historically accurate, in some instances even more so than the synoptic gospels, it is still true that John is definitely more interested in a theological or spiritual understanding of what Jesus says and does than he is in presenting an accurate chronology. The two, however, need not be mutually exclusive, and in John they are not!

John begins his Gospel not as Mark did with Jesus' baptism, not as Matthew with his genealogy, not as Luke with Jesus' birth; John starts before the creation of the world. "In *the beginning was the Word, and the Word was with God, and the Word was God. He was in the beginning with God. All things came into being through him, and without him not one thing came into being. He was in the world, and the world came into being through him; yet the world did not know him. He came to what was his own and his own people did not accept him. But to all who received him, who believed in his name, he gave power to become children of God, who were born, not of blood or of the will of the flesh or of the will of man, but of God.*" (1:1 ff) To say the least, this is theological, and yet no more theological than the other Gospels. We will see this later in close examination of the birth and resurrection narratives. John did carefully craft his Gospel to be a seamless creation, just as Jesus' robe, woven of one piece. John would not have looked kindly upon the effort of the scholars of the historical quest for Jesus to peel away the layers of his Gospel, as if it were an onion, in an effort to get back to the actual historical situation. Thankfully John did not have to voice this complaint, for the scholars simply ignored John as not being historical and left him in peace.

There is also a great irony in the view of those German scholars which seemed to have eluded all those who did not accept John's gospel as historically accurate. John Zebedee, the apostle, was considered by the early church to be the author of the Gospel of John, and scholars have generally agreed this is true or true for the largest part of the Gospel. The irony, then, is that this fact makes John's Gospel the closest eyewitness to Jesus and to the events in Jesus' life! And John is the only Gospel which does claim, and if John Zebedee is the author, CAN claim, to be written by a disciple! Would not that make his account the most historical? You would think so, but nonetheless until recently, scholars ignored John as historically unreliable, in favor of the synoptic gospels. Probably not the most correct choice, but a choice did, does, have to be made. The incidents in Jesus' ministry and the chronology of his ministry are simply dramatically different in the synoptic gospels and in John.

For example,

1. The synoptic gospels say repeatedly that Jesus spoke in parables ...but John doesn't have even one parable.
2. Only John includes Jesus' miracles of water into wine and the resurrection of Lazarus. Only John relates the story of the woman taken in adultery and those beloved words of Jesus, "Whoever is without sin cast the first stone..."
3. And who is right, Mark who places the whole of Jesus' ministry into one year, or Matthew and Luke who indicate perhaps a year and a half, or John who says a definite three years?
4. And did Jesus visit Jerusalem once as the synoptic gospels say, or four times as John says?
5. Unlike the other three, in John's gospel Jesus from the beginning of his ministry knows himself to be the Christ. Jesus is also at once most divine and most human, with emotions from anger to grief: he took a whip to the temple sales force, wept at Lazarus' tomb, cried out on the cross, and died a brutal death. Jesus is God, yet as human as one can be.

Many criticize the 'I am" sayings of Jesus in John as interpretations, not what Jesus actually said. To be sure it is very likely not exactly what

Jesus said, but we really don't know what Jesus actually said! Matthew, Mark and Luke are not necessarily closer to the real words of Jesus just because they record shorter more pithy sayings. Of the four gospels John is the only one which claims to be written by an eyewitness to Jesus' words, and may be paraphrasing what he remembered Jesus saying. The other three were choosing from oral sources or remembrances of others. None of them had a definitive verbatim account of Jesus' words.

Still it is a perplexing question why only John tells of the raising of Lazarus, the water to wine miracle at the Cana wedding, and the beautiful story of the woman caught in the act of adultery. These three are such big deals that if the other Gospels knew of them, surely they would not have omitted them. Which raises the question; did they know of them? Why does only John include them? And the bigger question, did they really happen, or is it a literary device of John? In this regard, remember John is the only Gospel that claims first hand personal contact with Jesus. The other three do not. John asserts particulars of topography and chronology the others do not seem to know, and which modern archaeological discoveries have verified. John is very concerned with dates and places, distances and names of towns and so on. He includes hundreds of such references. Matthew and Luke tend not to know these things or to choose not to include them, and on some occasions get them wrong. John was there, as we say, and they were not. This is also true of the crucifixion. John is the only one who stood at the foot of the cross, along with some of Jesus' female followers. The others had fled, or at best were at the fringe of the crowd. So they may not have seen what John says he saw: "...water and blood flow forth from Jesus pierced side." We cannot simply discard the possibility the other three gospel writers simply did not know of those incidents!

When you compare the four gospels, John shows the best and most accurate knowledge of Jewish customs, history, names, people and places. At the time of the gospels there was tremendous tension, even animosity, between northern and southern Palestine, that is between

Galileans and Judeans. John has all of that front and center, clear and strongly presented. The other three are not as clear about it. Another big question to ponder is, when the Gospels say Jesus' entry to Jerusalem on Palm Sunday was a triumphant entry, loudly hailed by the crowds of people, why did the people turn so quickly against Jesus at Pilate's trial? The synoptic gospels suggest the religious leaders turned the people against him. John presents a different very realistic view. He says the Palm Sunday experience was crowd fervor, hoping Jesus was the Messiah who would finally overthrow Rome. This messianic hope was a hot political agenda of the people, and they thought Jesus would be the one to lead them. When this didn't happen, when Jesus completely disavowed such aspirations, they abandoned him. This was true for even some of his followers who did the same.

John clearly insists eternal life does not begin after we die, but begins now as we become one in Christ, and then continues on through this life and after death. In this John and Paul agree, and they both disagree with the synoptic gospels which understand eternal life as beginning after death in the general resurrection. Not a small difference! Both John and Paul understand Life in Christ, to use Paul's phrase, to be an abundant life, filled with the Spirit, insight, understanding, love and forgiveness. It is a new life that is given in Jesus, and those who accept the invitation to follow him, even though still in this life, are also living in an alternate reality from the rest of the world. They remain **in** the world ... but are no longer truly or really **of** the world.

Organizationally, John's Gospel divides itself into five parts, not equal either in size or perhaps importance, but five divisions nonetheless.

1. The Prologue 1: 1-18
2. Narratives, Signs, Conversations 1:19-12:50
3. Jesus Alone with His Disciples 13:1-17:26
4. The Passion and Resurrection 18:1-20:31.
5. The Epilogue 21: 1-15.

1. In the prologue John presents Jesus as the Word of God made flesh. Jesus was with God, was God from the beginning of time; but moved by love for the world and the need to bring justice; God comes into the world in his Son Jesus. John the Baptist calls Jesus the Lamb of God. Then Jesus calls four disciples. (1:19-51)

2. In chapters 2-12 John presents seven signs which Jesus did, only two of which, feeding the five thousand and walking on water, are included in the Synoptic Gospels. John has five signs the others do not include, all of which witness to who Jesus is; and in all of them some believe and some do not. Another difference between the Gospels is that for John Jesus' ministry was primarily in Jerusalem and for the others it was in Galilee. John also differs considerably from the others in recording four visits of Jesus to Jerusalem, not just one; and Jesus' disruption of the temple begins at the start of his ministry in John, not as in the others at the end of it.

3. Many have noticed that there seems to be a dramatic shift in John's Gospel in chapters 13 to 17. He moves away from trying to convince readers that Jesus is the Messiah toward affirming Jesus' identity with the community of faith and the importance of community membership; because it is in service of each other that the presence of Christ within us is shown. Jesus washes the disciples' feet, the role of a servant, and commands the disciples to "Love one another as I have loved you." Since only God can give commandments, John is saying again Jesus IS God. He quotes Jesus as saying "I am the Way, the Truth and the Life" and exhorts his followers to abide in him as the branches to the vine. Then Jesus promises to send the Holy Spirit to lead them.

4. Chapters 18-20 take place during the last week of Jesus' life, between Palm Sunday and Good Friday. The arrest, crucifixion and resurrection comprise the last chapters of John.

5. Chapter 21. The disciples are back at the Sea of Galilee. It is very interesting that they have gone home, back to doing what they did before their ministry with Jesus; they are fishing again. The narrative says they had worked through the night and caught nothing. Jesus appears, and they catch 153 fish. A very similar story is found in Matthew 4:18–22, Mark 1:16–20 and Luke 5:1–11; however the event is placed at the beginning of Jesus' ministry, not after the resurrection. John's version is quite different from the others also in the fact that Jesus grills the fish they caught and they have breakfast. Then Peter is grilled as well, as Jesus pointedly brings up his denials in the courtyard! The death of both Peter and the beloved disciple are foretold. The final sentence pretty much echoes the close of the Gospel in chapter 20.

We cannot leave John without briefly considering those three stories only John includes in his Gospel: the wedding at Cana, the woman caught in adultery, and the raising of Lazarus. All three are highly metaphoric expositions by John. To whatever extent they do relate historical incidents; they have been completely redone by John to serve his overarching purpose of demonstrating that Jesus is the Son of God, Messiah and Savior.

The wedding in Cana (John 2:1-12) is a good illustration of John's method or intention for all three of these unique stories, all of which are said by John to be "signs" which demonstrate God's presence in Jesus, even as he also insists the ability to see or understand that this is true is given only to those whom the Spirit has given the eyes to see it as such. Therefore, some do; and some do not.

The water into wine sign at Cana, of all Jesus' signs, has perhaps troubled readers of John's gospel more than any other. Why in the world would Jesus create 120 gallons of wine? Why such an excess, and why so late in the wedding, when, as the steward said, they were already somewhat drunk. The answer is Jesus didn't...not exactly. Let us reprise the story. John says six water jars, each holding twenty to thirty gallons of water, were present to be used for the Jewish rites of purification. That is, it was used for the Jewish rites of the old covenant, which was being superseded in Jesus. Jesus tells them to fill the water jars to the brim. He wants it to be clear the rites of purification are being scrupulously observed. They fill the jars, and then Jesus says, "Draw some out and take it to the steward." Ok, the inference is that since something happened to the water, which somehow became wine, that Jesus did it. But John does not make that claim. What John says is that the water in the jars, the water of the Jewish purification rites, in other words the old covenant, was drawn out and taken to the steward who exclaims, "You have kept the good wine until now." What John intends, what he is saying in this story, is that in Jesus God has totally changed everything. The old covenant has become the new wine of the covenant in Jesus. Jesus is the fulfillment of the old covenant; the purification rites are valid no more, for in Jesus everything is changed. In Him "The good wine," is now here!

John's story was understood as he intended within the early community. The church fathers realized that John was using allegory and metaphor to make his point. They recalled that in the Jewish scripture, which was also Jesus' scripture, the metaphor of a "wedding" is often used by the prophets to describe the relationship of God with his people. A wedding, wine and vineyards were often used as symbols for the reign of God or the kingdom of God. We need to ask; could all of this have been in the mind of John as he wrote his Gospel and remembered the wedding he had attended with Jesus in Cana? Was that also perhaps the reason why Jesus often referred to himself as "the bridegroom?" Whatever actually happened in that wedding, it was for the disciples their first event with Jesus; and it was a powerful experience, so much so it convinced the disciples who he was, strengthened their faith; and John says the disciples "believed in him."

John puts the story right at the start of Jesus' ministry to make clear that in His person, in who He was, and what He was doing, the power of God was present in Jesus. John could well have added here the words of

Jesus to Nathaniel just before the wedding: "Greater things than this you will see." (1:50)

In similar manner the purpose of the story of the woman caught in adultery was to show that Jesus has the power to forgive sin. The purpose in the raising of Lazarus is seen in the exchange between Jesus and Martha. Jesus says, "I am the resurrection and the life, those who believe in me, though they die, will live. And everyone who lives and believes in me will never die. Martha, do you believe this?" (11:25). That exchange with Martha is the key to the whole event. John is saying those who are in Christ do not die. John shares with Paul the understanding that once we are called into fellowship with Jesus, we are "in Christ," as Paul put it, a phrase which means we partake right now in the future Jesus brings about in his resurrection. That future day of consummation is still to come, and yet, for us who are in Jesus, it is already a reality and hence we are right now living in eternal life and do not really die.

So the Gospel of John is interpreted history, written to prove, validate, what John passionately believed with all his heart; that Jesus of Nazareth who lived and died in Palestine was not only a man but the very fullness of God present among us for the salvation of the world. To be sure, this is the same intention of all four Gospels--to show that Jesus is the Lord, Son of God, Savior, the fulfillment of God's plan, worked out through the history of his people, the Jews. And as we will see, all four Gospels use the same method to convey this incredible truth...story, myth, and metaphor...the only means which really can capture, or try to capture, explain or relate, the incredible truth that they experienced and knew to be reality, that Jesus who was dead had been raised from the dead, thus proving his claims, and bringing the power of his life to all who live in him. John is not unique in using metaphor and symbol, but he is a master of it!

Chapter Thirteen

Paul

Between Jesus' resurrection and Mark, the first Gospel, is a gap of at least 20 years. That gap increases for Matthew and Luke to 30 or more years. Not a long time, and yet, a time sufficient to cast a bit of uncertainty or cloudiness over exactly what Jesus had said and done and how it was to be understood. That fact, plus the many differences in the four Gospel accounts of Jesus and his ministry, raised many questions. Who would settle those questions? On what authority would they be settled? This was the problem with which the growing community had to wrestle. It was a huge difficulty. We will see in later chapters how the church dealt with this.

Paul however does not suffer from a time gap. Nor is Paul writing an account of Jesus' ministry. The crucifixion is basically thought to have taken place in the years 32-35. Paul's conversion experience on the road to Damascus can be dated between 33 and 36, about a year after the resurrection. So Paul's experience, which he relates in his letters, is one of the earliest accounts we have of Jesus' resurrection appearance. And the letters of Paul are also the earliest Christian documents we possess. Paul's letter to the Thessalonians about the year 50 is most likely his first letter, and thus our earliest written document. Paul says the tradition within the community is the source for his understanding of Jesus. That means Paul relied upon those same oral remembrances and stories upon which the Gospels relied. However, unlike the Gospels, Paul does not relate the experiences of others. He insisted that he had a direct visitation of the Lord. He based his teaching and his authority for teaching it upon his experience of Jesus on the road to Damascus, and upon other occasions. Paul insisted there was no uncertainty at all that his authority came from the Lord. And therefore, on that basis, what he taught was right and true.

The story of Paul's conversion from Saul the persecutor of Christians into Paul the missionary to the Gentiles is a story told three times in the book of Acts. (9:1-19, 22: 3-21, 26: 1-18) Luke was a traveling companion with Paul for a time, and might very well have gotten the story of the Damascus road experience directly from Paul. In the chapter 22 version Paul tells of the event in his own words: *"While I was on my way and approaching Damascus, about noon a great light from heaven suddenly shone about me. 7 I fell to the ground and heard a voice saying to me, 'Saul, Saul, why are you persecuting me?' 8 I answered, 'Who are you, Lord?' Then he said to me, 'I am Jesus of Nazareth whom you are persecuting.' 9 Now those who were with me saw the light but did not hear the voice of the one who was speaking to me. 10 I asked, 'What am I to do, Lord?' The Lord said to me, 'Get up and go to Damascus; there you will be told everything that has been assigned to you to do.' 11 Since I could not see because of the brightness of that light, those who were with me took my hand and led me to Damascus.*

While some critics doubt the account in Acts, based upon Luke's penchant for the supernatural and miraculous, whatever actually happened Paul experienced a spiritual visitation of the risen Jesus. In his comments in two of his letters, while he does not discuss his experience in detail, he does refer to the experience. To the Corinthians, after relating the resurrection appearances of Jesus to the disciples, he says "Last of all, as to one untimely born, he appeared also to me." (1 Cor. 15:3–8) In his letter to the Galatians Paul says "I want you to know, brothers and sisters that the gospel I preached is not of human origin. I did not receive it from any man, nor was I taught it; rather, I received it by revelation from Jesus Christ." (1:11-16)

Contrary to the account in Acts, Paul says that his experience of the risen Jesus was something internal, a spiritual experience rather than an outward, physical and objective event. Since Luke traveled with Paul, it is very interesting that he nonetheless relates that a bright light, a voice, temporary blindness, were the means through which Paul experienced the risen Jesus, so powerfully he knew him to be the Son of God.

Regardless of both Luke's account and Paul's, there was uncertainty and a great deal of disagreement about Paul in the Jewish segment of the community. Jesus' brother James, the leader of the community in Jerusalem, opposed the whole notion of a mission to the Gentiles … which Paul understood to be his specific charge by Jesus in his vision. On the mission to the gentiles there was great disagreement, but there was none regarding the authority of Paul to teach.

This was neither a personal nor an isolated problem however. The community was dealing with many questions and concerns, and uncertainties abounded. To be sure the Resurrection proved God was present in Jesus. But in what way was God present in him? How was Jesus' relationship to the Holy Spirit to be understood? None doubted the reality of Jesus relationship to either God or the Holy Spirit, but the details of the relationship were uncertain. To deal with this question, the only authority available to them was;

1. The personal visitation of Jesus to the eye witnesses, the disciples and other followers of Jesus
2. The personal visitation of Jesus to Paul
3 The oral tradition.
4. The guidance of the Holy Spirit.

The problem was, exempting for now the Holy Spirit, these authorities often disagreed with each other, and in some cases were in complete contradiction. It was a situation like that well known story of three witnesses to an auto accident. One said the offending car was red, the second thought it was blue and the third was absolutely certain it was black. Who was right? Who was wrong? And who would be the one to separate the sheep from the goats? Paul, and the gospel of John, both agree Jesus was pre-existent in the mind and plan of God before his incarnation into human flesh. The synoptic Gospels do not make this assertion directly, but as we will see, in the stories regarding Jesus birth they basically did achieve much the same point of view.

However the early community was not homogeneous in its understanding, and some, mostly on the fringe of the community, but still part of it, asserted that Jesus was only a man. He was beloved and "adopted" by God, but only a mortal as are all human beings. Others, equally more at the edge than the mainstream, claimed Jesus was indeed God, but only and completely God, not human in any way. He wore his humanity as one might put on a coat or a suit. He looked human but he was purely divine. This controversy continued to be hotly debate for the next 400 years. It wasn't until the Council of Chalcedon in 451 settled the debate in the doctrine of "The Two Natures of Christ," that Jesus was understood by the community as a whole to be true God and true man. But still, this was such a complicated theological and philosophical conclusion, such a deep problem to reconcile, that even the decision of the council contained within it enough ambiguity about the finer points involved to lead to a split between the Western and Eastern sections of the church 600 years later in 1054.

From the beginning the situation was volatile, uncertain and somewhat unclear because the picture of Jesus presented in the gospel accounts is that of a complicated man who did not provide an unambiguous definition of who he was. Jesus gave no particulars of theology; he simply proclaimed that in him God was present in a new and unique way, to bring about a whole new world. It was left up to the church and the Holy Spirit to fill in the how and why. The first efforts to do that, the first Christian writings we can date for sure, are Paul's letters to the congregations which he had founded. But Paul's conversion experience is dated to AD 33–36, and his first letter to the year 50. What happened in those years in between?

Paul says clearly that after his experience of Jesus on the Damascus road he did not consult with "anyone" (Galatians 1: 12-16) He specifically did not go to Jerusalem to see the disciples, or the community of believers, but went to Arabia, and then returned to Damascus. It seems Paul wants it to be clearly understood he did not seek either advice or consultation from the community in Jerusalem. It is reading between the lines, but considering Paul's later difficulties with the Jerusalem group, he may have had reason not to go there. Paul does not elaborate on why he went to Arabia or what happened there, but this may have been the occasion when he was taken to the third heaven, and experienced other visions of Jesus. Paul records this in his second letter to the Corinthians where Paul says, "I know a person in Christ who fourteen years ago was caught up to the third heaven—whether in the body or out of the body I do not know; God knows." (12:2) He wrote this around 53-56, so fourteen years earlier would put him in Arabia when it occurred. It seems Paul is either saying or implying that, when in Arabia, he was taught by the Lord. Beyond that Paul is quite tight-lipped about what went on in those years, and we have no other record about the event than his letters. The important thing about Paul's vision and his Arabia experience is that in his ministry he does not base his teaching of the faith upon the experience of others in the community. He insists that he had a direct visitation of the Lord, that his teaching comes from that experience, and therefore he had no uncertainty at all about that what he was teaching was right and true. He certainly taught it with power and conviction!

Chapter Fourteen

Example of Textual Development

In our previous chapters we took a general look at each Gospel, noting that they were written by an author who wrote with a purpose in mind and mainly for a special audience. Drawing heavily upon the oral tradition and Peter's eye-witness account, Mark wrote a short and to-the-point summary of Jesus as an evangelism tool for the early community. Matthew wrote primarily for the newly converted or interested Jews, and his purpose was to show Jesus fulfilled all the Old Testament requirements for the Messiah. Luke wrote for the Gentiles who were rapidly becoming the majority in the church. His purpose was to dispel the accusations that Jesus was crucified for treason to Rome and to show he was the savior of the whole world. John, the only Gospel written by a disciple, writes for the whole community to prove Jesus is the Savior, pre-existent in the mind and intention of God.

We look now at an example of how the different approach of each gospel puts its own "spin" on what is being said. They often make a subtle change to a story or incident so that it better meets the needs of their readers or their purpose in writing. In the following example each of the Gospels presents the same story told with just a touch of difference. (John doesn't relate this story.)

MARK

We will begin with Mark. The setting is Capernaum, at the very start of Jesus' ministry. A discussion takes place between some curious by-standers who ask Jesus why it is that the disciples of John the Baptist and the disciples of the Pharisees fast, but Jesus and his disciples do not. Jesus replies, "The wedding guests cannot fast while the bridegroom is with them, can they? As long as they have the bridegroom with them, they cannot fast. The days will come when the bridegroom is taken away from them, and then they will fast on that day." 2:19-20) Then Jesus comments as follows:

> *Mark 2:22 "And no one puts new wine into old wineskins; otherwise, the wine will burst the skins, and the wine is lost, and so are the skins; but one puts new wine into fresh wineskins."*

Mark quotes Jesus as saying, "New wine is for new skins!" What Jesus brought into the world was a new phenomenon, something that had never happened before. The teachings of Jesus, like new wine, required new skins to hold it. If the new reality that is Jesus would be put into the old forms, the old ways, that former understanding cannot contain it and it will burst at the seams!   The old must be put aside in order to embrace the new. It is the direct point of Mark that radical newness cannot be embraced within old attitudes. In Jesus everything has changed. And we must change with it. We can just feel the excitement which has burst into that early community with the resurrection of Jesus! It is a new world! But, as with everything new, this new way had to prove itself to those who held to the old ways. That's how it was then; that's how it still is. For them and for us, what we know is safe and comfortable; new things are unknown and scary. And even as they wanted to embrace Jesus and his message, many still tried to also cling to the old ways they had been taught. It was a dilemma, for the newness of the Gospel truly could not be contained within the old forms of Judaism. What God had done in Jesus was so radical it required a radically new understanding. Mark's account is straightforward and makes that point clearly. Jesus is new wine and requires a new wineskin.

MATTHEW

But true as Matthew knew this to be, even as he copied Mark his concern was to convince those Jewish Christians that, as Jesus had said, he did not come to abolish the old covenant, but to fulfill it. In a sense they were being asked to give up the old for the new and improved version, something they were reluctant to do because the "give-up" required putting aside what they had always believed to be sacred and true. Matthew wants them to understand that giving up need not be all that difficult, because actually Jesus is a new version of the old way, not a radical departure after all. In Jesus they can keep the best of what had been, and fill it out with the best of what in Jesus now is and would continue to be in the new covenant. Matthew was trying to have it both ways. So he adds to what Jesus said the words "so both are preserved."

> Matthew 9: 17 *"Neither is new wine put into old wine-skins; otherwise, the skins burst, and the wine is spilled, and the skins are destroyed; but new wine is put into fresh wineskins, **and so both are preserved."***

This is an editorial addition, as if Matthew asked himself, as he wrote many years later, "What would Jesus have said in the situation the church is in right now?"   Matthew concluded that if Jesus were there now, he surely would be sensitive to the needs of these Jews and would have said things in a less confrontational manner. This effort of Matthew to conciliate is also seen when Jesus says "Think not that I have come to abolish the law and the Prophets, I have come not to abolish them, but to fulfill them." 5:17) Only the gospel of Matthew records these words of Jesus.

So, having decided what Jesus would have said, Matthew has him say it: "...both are preserved," the old wine of Jewish heritage and the new wine of the Gospel. Matthew quickly discovered what every parish pastor learns in short order; you can't change the old ways too quickly. Even when things are changing all around you, even when it is clear the old ways need to adapt, still you have to be sensitive to those who cannot so readily do so. What this incident shows us is that the Gospel was beginning to see opposition from Jewish believers. While originally attracted to Jesus, many were reluctant to give up what they had been taught and the traditions in which they had always lived. It was a true dilemma for them. Sensitive to their situation, Matthew adds that conciliatory note that even as we adopt the new ways, the old ways, the Jewish heritage from the past, need not be obliterated. It will remain, fulfilled and better than ever. Matthew's addition was surely a sweet word to the ears of those reluctant Jewish Christians!

However, Matthew's well-intentioned tinkering with what Mark recorded also gave encouragement to those Jewish Christians who adamantly insisted that the old needed to be observed in its entirety! That it was necessary, not only to keep the old ways, but also to enforce them upon all new members of the community. This viewpoint, which came to be largely centered with James and his leadership in Jerusalem, while received positively by the Christians in Jerusalem, created huge problems for Paul's mission to the Gentiles.

LUKE

Luke's Gospel was written a few years after Matthew and shows how the new wine/old wine difficulty, the need to keep "kosher," or the freedom to abandon it, continued in the community. However, Luke wrote to the Gentiles, an entirely different group of believers than those for whom Matthew had written, and in the Gentile world the problem was exacerbated. Newly converted to Christianity they did not know anything about those Jewish traditions, nor did they care about them! As they read Matthew's solution to the new wine problem, they were unimpressed.

They asked, "Why must we do what Matthew says? And how do we hold to both the old and the new?" They said, "It's a nice sentiment, something nice to say, but the truth is the old ways are no longer relevant outside the Jewish community." They understood that it was tradition and heritage for Jewish Christians to be circumcised, to keep a kosher kitchen, to obey purification rituals, and so on; and it was fine for them, but these things made no sense to Gentile Christians. "Why," they asked, "should we have to be circumcised? That's an old wineskin. And why should we follow Jewish dietary laws? That too is old thinking." In other words, "Why do we have to drink the new wine out of the old wineskins? Even Jesus said the new is better." These strong and valid questions were asked by the Gentiles, who were rapidly becoming the majority in the community. For them the original words of Jesus made the most sense; the new wine of the Gospel needed a new wineskin.

So the fledgling church was faced with an evangelism problem. They would never attract or keep Gentiles if they insisted upon Jewish requirements. Maybe it was this practical truth as much as anything, but a choice had to be made, and the church went with the new. They went with Mark, whose version was actually the original. They did not choose Matthew, and predictably, although not for this reason alone, the Jewish Christians dropped out. They stopped pledging, stopped attending; some of them gathered into a kind of Jewish-Christian community; some went back to the temple. This way of handling things, to just pick up your stuff and leave, is familiar to any member of a church!

But this reaction perplexed the Gentile Christians, who could not understand why their Jewish brethren had to be so hard-headed. Why did they insist on being stuck in the old ways when it was obvious the teachings of Jesus were radically new and different? The Gentiles said of the Jews in those early congregations all the same things we still say today whenever we agree with a proposal for change and someone else doesn't. They are hard-headed! So in response to his Gentile converts, Luke adds to Mark's original:

*Luke 5: 39 "And no one puts new wine into old wine-skins; otherwise the new wine will burst the skins and will be spilled, and the skins will be destroyed. But new wine must be put into fresh wineskins. **And no one after drinking old wine desires new wine, but says, 'The old is good.'"***

Those words at first reading seem to be commending the old wine, saying it is better. But Luke would never contradict Jesus who said the new was better, and such a conclusion would not serve his evangelism to the Gentiles. What seems most likely is that Luke is here explaining to the perplexed Gentiles why the Jews left, because they are lovers of the old tradition. They preferred the old wine. They feel the old is better. At the same time it was well known then as now that new wine is never as good when it is new as it is when it has had some time to age. Since a new wine may well turn out to be a fantastic vintage given time, Luke could also be saying that while the new is rejected by those who feel more comfortable with the old, they will discover that the new will ultimately turn out to be a much better wine.

Now, if it is correct (as I believe) that John's gospel was written very early, and was one of the gospels included by Luke in his listing of "others who have written," then Luke would be aware of John's gospel, perhaps have a copy of it in front of him as he wrote. If so, and really even if not, Luke may have had in mind the tradition in the community regarding the wedding in Cana. The water in the stone pots, used for the Jewish rite of purification, was given to the wine steward, who offered the pronouncement that the "best had been saved until last." The new wine of the Gospel, the wine of the Lord's Supper, the wine of the "new covenant," is a better wine than that of the former covenant, the old covenant of Moses. (See John 2: 1-11)

The intention of this comparison is to help us realize the creative way in which the Gospel writers applied the teachings of Jesus to the needs of evangelism and teaching in their faith communities. That they did this with startling freedom is another insight for us in how we should interpret and read Scripture for the needs and situations of our day! The New Testament is not merely a holy collection of books to be revered because they are hallowed or ignored because they no longer apply to our lifestyle. Rather it is a book with which we must enter into dialogue and seek to discover what it says to our world view, our attitudes, priorities and opinions. I will argue this more forcefully in later chapters.

The little story of the wine and wineskins also illustrates for us why and how it is that different Christians come to different conclusions in matters of faith. Some, then and today, understand the New Testament as the "Word of God," in the sense that what is written must be read and understood as it is written, which is an "old wineskin" point of view. Others would ask, "Whose words-- Mark's, Luke's or Matthew's?" This is more the new wineskin approach in which those issues, a closed door to some, are an open door to further debate.

This is a way to say that, as we read the New Testament and seek to understand what it says, we do so in a time and place quite different from that of the first century. The 21st century possesses medical, scientific and other knowledge the first century did not even dream could be! We cannot ignore those aspects of our world view which give us insight to life and understanding of creation and reality, which they did not possess in the first century. But we must be careful not to assume that, therefore, the first century stories are inferior and no longer relevant to our time and place. Perhaps this is another reason the Gospels are written in metaphor and symbol which endure and apply in every culture and for every generation. Christians have always approached the Bible with different methodologies. We could say now, as then, some prefer the old, some prefer the new. Matthew would say that's fine...there is room for both. Maybe that is why Matthew is still the favorite of the four Gospels!

Chapter Fifteen

Beginning of the Canon

It wasn't until the year 394 that the New Testament as we know it, the books as we have them, were collected and formally approved by the church. Until then there were strong and often acrimonious differences of opinion as to which writings were Scripture and which were not. Many holy writings of advice and counsel circulated among the churches of the Empire which were held in high regard as "writings," but which, with slight exception, were not regarded as Scripture." Collected by the church, they were held in high esteem as the writings of the Apostolic Fathers. Other writings, claiming to be written by Paul, Peter, Phillip, Thomas or one of the other disciples, were not so highly regarded. Still, they claimed for themselves the same authority as the Gospel writers, and who was to say? Scholars generally call these non-canonical writings "apocryphal," meaning they are of questionable authority or, as Webster defines the word, "unlikely to be true." However I prefer to call these writings "alternative" gospels. It seems less confusing and a better term because they were, at the time, alternatives to the books which **were** chosen for inclusion in the New Testament Canon. And in some parts of the community, many were considered to be authentic. The Holy Spirit did not choose to include them in the 27 approved books, but the influence of these writings upon the developing community is undeniable.

As commented earlier, Acts 2:42-47 tells us the early Christian community was a golden age, in which all shared their goods in common, loved one another, and went about life with joy and friendly persuasion. Luke was perhaps embellishing things for Theophilus because the alternative Gospels show us a different reality, in which there was no unanimity of opinion at all, even in the very beginning. The early community was at least as diverse as it is today and every bit as divisive. The alternative writings comprise an amazing number of stories about Jesus and collections of sayings of Jesus. These "gospels," as they describe themselves, have been found in some cases almost in their entirety, in others only in large fragments or small pieces. Some are only mentioned in other writings which quote from them or refer to the content, or to the name, or to the title of the writing.

The importance of these gospels and writings--when they were written, where, and for what purpose--is a matter of continuing serious study and debate among scholars. It is obvious in some instances that the writings are patent fabrications, perhaps even deliberately divisive, many written at a late date in the development of the New Testament. It is equally certain that at least some of these writings date from either a time contemporary to the writing of the canonical gospels or before. Because they represented a view that was not congenial to the main thought of the developing church, they were destroyed or suppressed. Some of these writings are complete documents, with a beginning, middle and ending. Some are more like short stories, neither detailed enough nor long enough to count as a real gospel. Some are a simple collection of things Jesus is supposed to have said. A category pretty much unto itself, a group called "the infancy gospels," purports to relate incidents in the boyhood life of Jesus, all of which are quite fanciful in content.

We will look at three of these gospels as representative of the genre, but first we need an orientation to the situation which existed when these alternative gospels circulated. It is important to understand the circumstances which created their writing and subsequent suppression. Just as today, human enterprise is always conditioned by what is possible, and compromise is usually a part of it. That was equally true in the selection of the Canon of Scripture. Of course, a process of compromise always raises the big and fundamentally important question; was the truth or purity of the message maintained? Or was it diluted, changed or even lost? I think you will find the answer to that, as well as the whole process of selecting the books of the New Testament, to be a fascinating adventure.

So here is the situation in which the believing community found itself as the first century ended. The teachings of Jesus, his life and deeds, were at first oral traditions and teachings, not written down, because the thrust of the church was to proclaim what God had done in Jesus. Anyhow the disciples and eye witnesses were still around to be consulted if needed. It was also thought the coming of the kingdom was just around the corner, so there was little pressing need for a written account.

Then, as the growing community demanded to know more about Jesus, Mark, Matthew, Luke and John beautifully undertook that task. At the same time, other gospels were also being written by authors claiming to be credentialed followers of Jesus. As it was usually obvious that they were not as they claimed to be, it raised the question of what should be done with these spurious writings? While some of the communities among the early church held them in high regard and thought they should be included in the Canon, the majority was adamantly opposed to that in any manner. The situation was ripe for confusion and desperate for some method of determining which of these writings were truly inspired and therefore legitimate, and which were not.

A definite and agreed upon scripture was badly needed, but equally pressing was the need for a standardization of theology and doctrine (which varied considerably among the wide spread communities), a system for organization and a catechism or compendium of basic beliefs, a uniform expression of the faith with which to teach the many who were flocking into the community. In a real sense Paul started this process in his letters to the earliest Christians, answering questions about the proper practice of the Lord's Supper, about marriage, baptism, food sacrificed to idols, resurrection, the second coming, and a myriad of practical organizational matters.

These essential needs of the church for organization, agreed theology, and, most of all, for an approved Scripture were developing simultaneously. The Hebrew Scriptures (Old Testament), the oral traditions, the letters of Paul, the Gospels, the alternative writings, and the letters and opinions of the Apostolic Fathers were the main sources for the theological principles the church used to shape what was to become the True Faith. In deciding which writings should be admitted or eliminated from the approved list, called "The Canon," the church applied a twofold requirement. Firstly, the author had to be an apostle or in close association with an apostle, for it was to the apostles that Jesus had committed the proclamation of the Gospel. The second requirement was that the writing in question must teach what was consistent with all the known apostolic writings; that is, did it proclaim the same faith, and in doing so, did it evidence being inspired by the Holy Spirit. Some of the books later to be included in the Canon--James, the Epistle to the Hebrews, and the second letter of Peter--were considered by many of the early church leaders not to have been written by the supposed author and thereby disqualified for inclusion in the Canon. These writings did fulfill the second requirement, however; and the ultimate decision was that they should be included. It is interesting that recent scholarship agrees that Paul did not write Hebrews, and Peter did not write Second Peter.

As the mid-second century arrived, there was strong agreement as to which Gospels fit this criterion and which did not; and the list of approved books was substantially finished by the year 200. However, because the community was so widespread, and travel so difficult, the list did not achieve immediate agreement. That was not achieved, and the Canon was not officially approved until the Council of Carthage in 394. And even then, while the Western church selected the 27 books we have in the New Testament today; in the Greek or Eastern part of the empire, 1 Clement, Barnabas, and the Shepherd of Hermes, were included in the New Testament as canonical writings and Revelation was eliminated. (Eventually Revelation was accepted) It was a muddy process, and while from a 21st century perspective, we may judge the two criterion and the process of selecting the books as being somewhat naive, the positive assessment is that it did determine the composition of the New Testament as we know it and settled that basic necessity.

However, there was a huge negative side as well. The process of creating a church organization, agreed dogma, and the Canon was difficult and contentious. It destroyed, ostracized, discredited and damned all opinions counter to the one which was rapidly becoming the "orthodox faith!" The discredited writings and competing viewpoints had to be dealt with; and to assure that the church would not continually fight the same old battles over and over again, the alternative writings which had been judged "heresy" were ordered to be destroyed. This edict was not, never could have been, completely effective; and some texts survived the official condemnation and the systematic burning and destruction. A sizeable collection of alternative texts were buried by an unknown person who was to become a great benefactor to many generations far in the future. This valuable "buried treasure" (literally!), is called the Nag Hammadi texts, after the town in Upper Egypt where they were discovered in 1945. This is the same year as the discovery of the Dead Sea Scrolls, and they were soon to play an equally important part in understanding the early Christian community.

The faith of the apostles and those followers contemporary with Jesus who followed him through his ministry or who knew those who did, testified to Jesus as the true revelation of God. Jesus was the "One" who alone fulfilled God's plan from creation. Jesus was the one whom the Old Testament prophecies foretold, the lamb who bore the sins of the world to the cross, the one who atoned for all humanity. Jesus was the only Son of God, the very incarnation of God in human flesh. God raised him from the dead and he appeared too many. This was the earliest faith.

But during the second and third centuries, all of these assertions were challenged or modified by those who, while considering themselves

Christian, held more conservative or more liberal views of who Jesus was, why he died, what his death meant, where and how he was born, and when or if he would indeed come again. The essential questions of every investigative reporter, "Who, what, why, when and where," were raised about the very basics of the faith. The first centuries were a complicated time for the church, filled with both great opportunity and perilous threat. The faith in Jesus literally burst upon a world of decaying belief in pagan rites, and a reluctant but progressive disillusion with Greek philosophy. It was as if a new creation was indeed dawning, as the Gospels said, and was sweeping away the past which was no longer viable.

But, as it was happening, it was neither that clear nor that certain what it was that was happening! It was a confused and foggy time, but it was also one in which the Gospel proclamation found immediate and enthusiastic reception. The counterattack of the dying world view, that last gasping effort to hold to what had always been true, the persecution of Rome, could not stop what was happening. The Gospel was on the march. Faith in the resurrection of Jesus, and through him the resurrection of all who were in Christ, seemed to be an irresistible force.

The one potential immovable object which might have stopped this seemingly irresistible march of the faith was not the persecutions of Rome, which were sporadic, usually localized and simply shrugged off. The blood of the martyrs joined with the blood of Jesus and lifted the church to ever increasing growth. The real threat to the developing church were the views alternative to the faith of the Apostles and the Gospels, which while in many ways very attractive, held within them a potentially fatal poison for Christianity. Gnosticism, as we have seen, and the alternative writings to which we turn next, presented for the most part such a complete distortion of the apostolic faith, that had they not been aggressively opposed, may have completely destroyed the church. That danger was real, but it was confusing and difficult to combat, because the lines of disagreement between the various groups were often blurred or overlapping. The church simply had to take a hard line, had to develop a hierarchy of authority, had to determine once and for all what the true

New Testament writings were. Much of the richness of the early community was lost in doing this; but truly it had to be done.

It is not within our scope or ability to discuss the alternative writings in detail, but for those who are interested, there is one terrific internet site available: *www.gnosis.org the Hag Hammadi site.* This is a great place to more intensely examine the alternative texts.

We now take a general look at three of those writings judged by the church to be heretical.

Chapter Sixteen

Alternative Gospels to the Canon

We will look at three samples of the alternative texts, which are representative of the genre.

In 1945, near the town of Nag Hammadi in Upper Egypt, an Arab peasant discovered a buried earthenware jug containing leather bound papyrus folios and some loose pages. By devious and exciting means, undoubtedly involving the black market and bribery, 52 alternative gospels and writings eventually came to the Coptic Museum in Cairo where they are still preserved. Others somehow disappeared since their discovery in 1945. The following three is illustrative of the whole group. (all *documents from www.gnosis.org the Hag Hammadi site*)

1. Gospel of Phillip probably written   180-350
This is an example of a later writing which was not in contention for inclusion in the New Testament, which had been basically assembled by the time this "gospel" of Phillip was written. It is not really a gospel except for its title, and, more than anything else resembles a Gnostic version of the more orthodox catechisms from the second through fourth centuries, explaining the significance of sacramental rites of initiation and the meaning of sacred names. It was an easy matter for the community to discard this writing as superfluous, but to what extent does it capture the thinking which also existed in the community at the time? The answer to

that question is Phillip's value for scholars. The only copy of this gospel is the one found at Nag Hammadi. It is written in Coptic but is obviously a copy from Greek. The claim to fame for the gospel of Phillip is the source material it gave to Dan Brown's speculations about Jesus' relationship with Mary Magdalene in his best-selling novel "The Da Vinci Code." The idea that they were married comes from two quotations in the gospel, although parts of the quotation are illegible or missing:

> *There were three who always walked with the Lord: Mary, his mother, and her sister, and Magdalene, the one who was called his companion. His sister and his mother and his companion were each a Mary. And the companion of the [...] Mary Magdalene. [.Jesus?}..] loved her more than all the disciples, and used to kiss her often on her mouth. The rest of the disciples [...]. They said to him "Why do you love her more than all of us?" The Savior answered and said to them, "Why do I not love you like her? When a blind man and one who sees are both together in darkness, they are no different from one another. When the light comes, then he who sees will see the light, and he who is blind will remain in darkness."*

Rather cryptic to most of us, but Brown's wonderful imagination took off from there and he wove a thriller about the marriage of Jesus and Mary and the founding of a family dynasty. A similar idea was used in the "Temptation of Christ" by Nikos Konstantinos, who suggests that Jesus, while in delirium on the cross, dreams that if he did come down he and Mary could have a life together. Is it worth it to die, Jesus asks himself. It is a powerful story, but if we put aside such speculation, the main value of the gospel of Phillip is the picture it gives us of the importance of Mary Magdalene in the early Christian Community. Indeed, from this and other alternative writings, we see that women in general played a much more important role in the early church than what the developing orthodoxy was to allow them. In fact later orthodoxy would not even admit woman had ever played a major role at all! A kind of misogyny had come into the church by the third century which was not present in the early community. Thank you Phillip for that correction and enlightenment!

2. Gospel of Thomas   50-150

This gospel is a good example of what is possibly a very early alternative writing. Not written by the Apostle Thomas, the true author of this gospel is unknown. This gospel is very different in tone and structure from other alternative gospels, and even more different from the four Canonical Gospels. It consists of a series of sayings attributed to Jesus. There is no mention of crucifixion or resurrection which could argue for the earlier date. If it does pre-date the Canonical gospels, it raises the exhilarating possibility that the gospel of Thomas is the elusive document "Q" which scholars are not certain ever existed. But what tantalizes is that, if it had, it would be a document very similar in form to Thomas, a collection of sayings of Jesus collected before his death. If indeed Thomas is a kind of diary, written during the ministry of Jesus, it would immediately move to the top of the list of important documents!

Of the 114 sayings in Thomas, 79 are in the four Canonical Gospels. We need to see a few examples for the possible importance of Thomas to become clear. The references are to stanzas in his gospel:

1. In Thomas (20) the disciples said to Jesus, *Tell us what the kingdom of heaven is like. "He said to them," It is like a mustard seed. It is the smallest of all seeds. But when it falls on tilled soil, it produces a great plant and becomes a shelter for birds of the sky.*

    Compare this to Mark 4: 30-31   (Jesus) said, *"With what can we compare the kingdom of God, or what parable will we use for it? It is like a mustard seed, which, when sown upon the ground, is the smallest of all the seeds on earth; yet when it is sown it grows up and becomes the greatest of all shrubs, and puts forth large branches, so that the birds of the air can make nests in its shade."*

2. In Thomas (34) Jesus said, *"If a blind man leads a blind man, they will both fall into a pit."*

   Compare Matt 15: 14 *Let them alone; they are blind guides of the blind. And if one blind person guides another, both will fall into a pit."*

3. In Thomas (64). Jesus said *"A man had received visitors. And when he had prepared the dinner, he sent his servant to invite the guests. He went to the first one and said to him, 'My master invites you.' He said, 'I have claims against some merchants. They are coming to me this evening. I must go and give them my orders. I ask to be excused from the dinner.' He went to another and said to him, 'My master has invited you.' He said to him, 'I have just bought a house and am required for the day. I shall not have any spare time.' He went to another and said to him, 'My master invites you.' He said to him, 'My friend is going to get married, and I am to prepare the banquet. I shall not be able to come. I ask to be excused from the dinner.' He went to another and said to him, 'My master invites you.' He said to him, 'I have just bought a farm, and I am on my way to collect the rent. I shall not be able to come. I ask to be excused.' The servant returned and said to his master, 'Those whom you invited to the dinner have asked to be excused.' The master said to his servant, 'Go outside to the streets and bring back those whom you happen to meet, so that they may dine.' Businessmen and merchants will not enter the places of my father"*

   Compare this to Luke 14: 16 -24 *Then Jesus said to him, "Someone gave a great dinner and invited many. At the time for the dinner he sent his slave to say to those who had been invited, 'Come; for everything is ready now.' But they all alike began to make excuses. The first said to him, 'I have bought a piece of land, and I must go out and see it; please accept my regrets.' Another said, 'I have bought five yoke of oxen, and I am going to try them out; please accept my regrets.' Another said, 'I have just been married, and therefore I cannot come.' So the slave returned and reported this to his master. Then the owner of the house became angry and said to his slave, 'Go out at once into the streets and lanes of the town and bring in the poor, the crippled, the blind, and the lame.' And the slave said, 'Sir, what you ordered has been done, and there is still room." Then the master said to the slave, 'Go out into the roads and lanes, and compel people to come in, so that my house may be filled. For I tell you, none of those who were invited will taste my dinner."*

The exciting possibility regarding the gospel of Thomas is that, even if it is not the source document "Q", it was written at a very early time, perhaps before, perhaps contemporaneous with the synoptic gospels. The exact dating is uncertain, some favoring closer to 50, others 150. Both are speculation, but it is a fascinating one!

3. Gospel of Mary 120 -180

This gospel was not discovered in Nag Hamadi but in a papyrus manuscript written in Coptic, discovered in 1896. Unfortunately the gospel is not complete, six pages from the beginning and an additional four in the middle are missing. The main importance of the Gospel of Mary, along with that of Phillip, is that they show leadership roles of women were commonplace and well regarded in early Christian communities. The growing orthodoxy challenged, even denied, that women had ever held positions of importance in the early church. Such a distortion required a vigorous defense, and the Gospel of Mary provides this defense, exalting Mary Magdalene over the male disciples of Jesus, and showing a strong position for women in the early church. Unfortunately the battle would be lost.

Why did the orthodox bishops relegate women to an inferior role in the community? After all, the gospels tell us women were the only disciples who did not scatter in fear after the trial of Jesus, but gathered around him at the foot of the cross and it was the women who were first to the tomb. It was also women who supported Jesus ministry, both with financial aid and general support. The alternative Gospels show us clearly how integral women were in the work of the church in its early centuries, and for this reason alone these alternative gospels are of tremendous value to the church. And, could it be, also one of the reasons the developing orthodoxy wanted them destroyed!

There were many tensions and difficulties in second-century community as they tried to reconcile the lesser role of women in Judaism with Paul's insistence on the equality of women with men, and the undeniable importance of women in Jesus ministry. Then, the whole debate was exacerbated by the developing orthodoxy, which denied both areas the alternative gospels show us were taken for granted in the early community: the validity of personal spiritual experience, and the authority of women to teach. By the late second century orthodoxy was well on the way to assuring that women would never again preach or administer the sacraments!

While it was the inexplicable misogynist views in an increasingly male dominated orthodoxy that caused the banning of the alternative gospels, in fairness there were other valid reasons as well. The theology of the alternative gospels is not in agreement with the canonical writings. In the gospel of Mary, Mary Magdalene is the Savior's beloved, who in good Gnostic style possesses knowledge and teaching superior to that of the apostolic tradition. Her superiority is based on private revelation, the "gnosis" of the gnostic movement, which is demonstrated in her capacity to strengthen the wavering disciples and turn them toward the Good. This Gnosticism was reason enough to ban the gospel.

But sadly, even though Jesus regarded women as equal in every way to men and counted as many females as males among his disciples, the view of the time that women were inferior soon began to assert itself in the developing church. Obviously the gospel of Mary was too dangerous to be allowed to circulate in the community and it was destroyed. Or so they thought. Happily it survived for a future generation to discover; and when put into the context of the first two centuries, it is a beautiful slam at the developing orthodoxy and its authority of bishops, all male, which

was coming into power and shutting women out of positions of authority. While their misogynist position was wrong, they rightly understood
that the alternative gospels often traveled down highly speculative, wildly
implausible, and basically pagan roads and it was completely necessary
they be banished from use in the church. On the other hand, perhaps
if those alternative views, so rich in diversity, had been allowed to continue in a process of dialog with the orthodox position, who knows what
insights might have developed? But that was not to be and in the next
chapters we look at how this played out.

Part Three

Moving into the World

Chapter Seventeen

Orthodoxy Wins!

So it was a difficult time--those first centuries--when the faith was taking shape, the New Testament being composed, and the doctrine and dogma of the church being put in place. As the early years moved into the 2nd and 3rd centuries, the tension between the alternative views of the faith and what was becoming the "true faith" developed into extreme partisan positions, with a first century equivalent to the hate e-mail, slogans, and 30-second political television ads we have all endured. But the developing orthodoxy had the upper hand; order is always preferred to chaos, and orthodoxy provided that order. Ironically, to achieve this they turned to pagan Rome as the model for the ecclesiastical structure of the church, and it turned out to be a brilliant move!

Following the Roman example, the power of bishops was enhanced and a primary bishop was selected. Then, using this new power, the bishops began to unify Christians isolated in various parts of the empire, not only under a central leadership, but also a required consistency of dogma and theology. The true faith was being hammered out, carefully and with precision, and the rationale for it was that if order was to prevail over chaos all views which contradicted or deviated from the growing definition of true Christianity must be suppressed.

"Orthodox" Christianity was beginning, even though in that beginning time not everyone agreed bishops should have such power over the community. While in retrospect they were perhaps right, those who opposed the growing power of bishops were a minority opinion, and orthodoxy soon developed a means to overcome the minority objection and secure its authority. The way to achieve this, while actually very simple, took decades to complete. First it was declared that only the bishops knew the true faith. This was later followed by acquiescing to the decision of Leo 1 (440-61) that the Bishop of Rome had authority over all the other bishops. Then, as if giving the final blessing to all that had gone before, it was asserted that the councils and bishops of the church alone have the authority to determine what Scripture is, what true doctrine is, and what true faith is. Even before this process was completed, those who disagreed with the bishops' decisions were pronounced "anathema" and asked to leave. As the centuries moved on, interdict, ex-communication, inquisition and martyrdom would be required of those who did not hold the orthodox view. Then the "coup de grace," to silence all who still might be tempted to disagree with the decisions of the bishops, it was finally determined that in matters of faith and order the "bishop of bishops," the Pope, is infallible. (First Vatican Council of 1870, Pope Pious IX)

The orthodox point of view triumphed, but from the beginning not everyone was comfortable with it; and even though the outward appearance might have indicated that a complete agreement was solidly in place that was not truly the case. The early communities' insistence on the Holy Spirit's personal witness as the source for certainty in matters of faith, not the pronouncements of bishops, had never completely left the church; and its continued presence, like a thorn in the flesh, eventually forced an ever increasing imposition of Papal authority, from Leo I (440-61) to the current Pope Francis (2013 --).

The early community's reliance upon the personal presence and witness of the Holy Spirit, which had remained throughout orthodoxy's march to power, proved to be the roots of, and impetus to, the reformation to come in the 15th century. Difficulties loomed on the horizon, no matter the apparent solid structure of "the true church," because no matter how strong, and how dominant Orthodoxy had become, it had begun in and remained a reactive or defensive position. The alternative views and insights of the earliest Christians it had sought to banish had not been destroyed after all, but in fact had imprinted upon the community the certainty that the Christian faith is not a matter of correct doctrine and proper authority, as the church was insisting.

So it was in many ways a sad story, in many ways an amazing one. But no matter how misguided it sometimes was it must be admitted that it is to the establishment of orthodoxy in the church and its organizational form, that we owe the very existence of the church. And perhaps those early orthodox Christians were right; and if the many views and multiple opinions which contended in the early years of Christianity had been allowed to remain and continue to contend, there could have been no cohesion and no uniformity to the faith. And it was that very (supposed) uniformity which, for good and for ill, is what attracted the Roman Emperor Constantine to the church. He needed something to help bond together the new Empire and saw the church as that glue. His decrees and efforts made that apparent uniformity of theology and agreement a reality and then imposed it unilaterally upon the Empire. In that sense Constantine truly was the champion of the Church.

It was with the Emperor's endorsement that what had once been a tiny Christian community centered in Jerusalem, persecuted, beleaguered, and nearly extinguished, as the 4th century ended, had achieved Empire-wide acceptance, and by the end of the 5th century was the official religion of the Roman Empire. The path to that point had been difficult, nourished with the blood of martyrs and continued conflict within the community, as faction fought faction. When orthodoxy became dominant and hierarchy the pattern for church administration, the church became less a community and more an institution. Not all were happy with this, and even as the cathedral of the church as institution was being built, cracks immediately began to appear around the edges of the foundation. Would it have toppled? Some say yes, and these are of the opinion that Constantine's intervention saved the church from itself, brought cohesion, and set it upon a strong foundation.

Yet the involvement of the state in the affairs of the church was at best a mixed blessing, and it can equally be argued that the baptizing of the Empire as "friend of the church" was really as much a danger as Gnosticism had been. Partnership with the Empire was even more alluring, offering everything the newly institutionalized church needed and wanted. Still, it was to be sure once again a Trojan horse. Fabulously so, for both the church and for the Empire, because hidden within this apparent common cause lurked the danger of worldly pride and riches for the church and loss of power and importance for the state. Present from the start, both were well hidden and that danger was not apparent, while the immediate benefit was, and it proved to be irresistible for church and state alike to refuse.

For the Emperor the blessing of the church, which by the 4th century was well entrenched in all parts of the Empire, gave a much needed cohesion to his rule of what truly was a disintegrating Empire. For the church, the endorsement of the Emperor promised protection rather than persecution, and prominence and social position for the clergy. Who could resist? Neither of them could resist. And, yet, should it not have been resisted? Could they not have found some accommodation that would better preserve the integrity of the Gospel even as the church embraced the support of the Empire? What might have been is not what happened. What did happen, what was to guide and determine the church for the coming 500 years, was in large part the legacy of one man, Gregory, called "The Great." Born about 540 he was elected Pope in 590. At his death in 604, he had determined, for better or worse, the direction of the church for generations to come. It was in many ways for the worst.

Deep in his heart Gregory shared some of the understandings of faith which had been deemed "heresy" in earlier generations. Specifically, Gregory held fast to the idea that the death of Jesus was not quite satisfaction enough for human sin. It seemed to Gregory that while baptism forgave the original sin, it was unable to penetrate to the depth of the sinful nature which continued to hold the human person in bondage. Gregory considered baptism powerful and effective, but, he asked, when the waters receded, did not a remnant of sin remain, unwashed, with residual power enough to incline us to the committing of new or additional sins? It seemed to Gregory the answer was yes. And for these new sins, would not God surely demand satisfaction beyond that of baptism? And how far realistically could even Jesus' death be stretched? After all, while Jesus' death took care of original sin, would not logic demand that something new had to be done to atone for new sins?

It seemed to Gregory, and too many others, that this was not only a reasonable point of view, but an obviously true one. Just look, they said, at the daily sins being committed by baptized persons! A theological problem! If new sins required new repentance, and new forgiveness, from where would this new forgiveness come? On what basis could the church again forgive sin after it had already applied the power of Christ's death in the washing of baptism? From where was an additional source of mercy and forgiveness to come? Gregory's concern about all this was not specifically answered, but it prepared the church for the late medieval idea of a "Treasury of Merit."

From the viewpoint of an organization which needed funds and support to continue its existence, the treasury of merit was a brilliant concept! This is how it was set up: it seemed reasonable to assume that if God mandated the living of a moral life and set down the parameters of what an acceptable moral life was, certainly some very holy people would exceed the basic requirements of God. In doing more than God required, would not extra credit be built up in God's eyes? Could not there not be a storehouse for this extra merit? Could not the church, controlling the storehouse, withdraw merit from it and apply it to others, thereby granting forgiveness for sins committed after baptism? It was a beautiful concept because it provided the church a way in which to forgive the new sins, as well as the manner in which forgiveness would be granted, thus also strengthening the power and authority of the church over all its members.

"The Great" Gregory also had a fondness for the miraculous, and his promoting of miracles as an activity of saints--and under some circumstances just plain heavenly intervention--led to miracles becoming nearly an everyday occurrence in later medieval faith. But while these new concepts did indeed add to the power and prestige of the institution, which was quickly becoming the Roman Catholic Church, it had very serious negative consequences for the Christian community as a whole. Under Gregory and succeeding Popes, the understanding of God's grace, which had been a personal and internal reality in the early community, became an external ceremony administered by the church by its own authority and power. Under Gregory the orthodoxy which had been developing in the early community, reached its first pinnacle; Christianity was now a powerful institution.

The views of Gregory remained the dominant understanding of Christianity in the western church for nearly 500 years, during which time there was little new theological development. Actually the Emperor Charlemagne (772 -814) was more dominant in the church during these years than the church hierarchy itself, whom Charlemagne treated with something just barely more than disdain. The church in his view was another of his servants.

Then in 795 the Cardinals chose Leo III as Pope (795-816), a choice which angered the political leadership of the church. Leo was from common origin, and up until then the papacy had been, and they felt should continue to be, reserved for those of more noble birth. The opposition to Leo's choice became violent and Leo had to appeal to the Emperor Charlemagne for protection. Ever since it had been put in place by Emperor Constantine, the agreed understanding was that the secular order, the Empire, held a superior position over the church; so when Leo appealed to Charlemagne, he was acting within this ancient "quid pro quo" arrangement. The Emperor protected the church; the church in return, as it had since Constantine, blessed Charlemagne's empire.

This was to completely change in the year 800 when Pope Leo III placed the crown of the Roman Empire on the head of Charlemagne! This was a dramatic and symbolic reversal of the previous subordinate role of the church. When the Pope conferred upon Charlemagne the authority to govern, he asserted the authority of the church over the emperor! What a reversal! What a great accomplishment for the little band of early Christians! Or was it?

Chapter Eighteen

Gregory VII and a New Era

The church, which at the time of Gregory V had worried about being incorporated into the empire and for 500 years was subordinate to the Empire, under Leo III began an era of papal supremacy which was to last more than another 500 years. Gregory VII (1073-1085) solidified the power of the church over the state by asserting that while the Pope can choose or depose princes and emperors, no one can depose the Pope who is appointed by God! The truth of Gregory VII's remarks was demonstrated in his famous confrontation with King Henry IV, The Holy Roman Emperor of the Germans. Henry insisted upon returning to the former superiority of the state over the church. Henry moved quickly on this, appointing the Bishop of Milan in 1075 and one year later forced a number of bishops in Germany to renounce allegiance to the Pope. Then Henry demanded the abdication of Gregory, who, not about to give up the power Leo had achieved, immediately responded by excommunicating Henry and deposing him from office effective one year later.

It was the princes of Germany who provided the political muscle Gregory needed, by refusing to accept Henry as the king as long as his excommunication remained in place. The princes gave Henry no choice; and in 1077 the Holy Roman Emperor of the Germans was forced to stand in the snow in Canossa until the Pope deigned to forgive him. The debate, actually a battle between church and state, continued with many steps forward and back for each side until the final conclusion occurred when Pope Innocent III (1198-1216) was able to say, "I rule the world!" And indeed he did. The Papacy was now the most powerful office in Europe.

But while it seemed the church had after all succumbed to the Trojan lure and was consumed with the pursuit of worldly power, the laity and the monasteries were rediscovering the piety and mysticism which had marked much of the early church. For more than a thousand years the faithful had done what they were told, believing what they were told to believe. The authority of the hierarchy-- Pope, priests, and church officials--was seldom doubted. The church ruled with the authority of God himself, claiming that it was the very presence of Christ on earth, and therefore the decrees of the church were inviolate. There was to be no discussion of this. It worked for centuries until suddenly it didn't, until suddenly there was a lot of discussion about it.

But it was too late, too much had changed, too much had happened; things could never really be the same as they had been. The community had become a "church," and the church had become an institution, and the institution had become a political power. It told kings where and when to kneel; it no longer was anything like it had been at the time of Paul, the apostles, the church fathers. As the newly rediscovered piety arose, it was held firmly within the hands of the institution. Unable to break from the authority of the institution, the renewed piety found its expression in a manner that could be approved by the church; pilgrimages and the adoration of relics.

Travel agents made fortunes as pilgrims sought out holy places. The Holy Land was first on the list, but also sites where miracles were said to have taken place, or where relics could be seen and venerated. Rome, the holy sites of Rome, were popular, as were the relics of Rome; a piece of bread from the Last Supper, a piece of the cross of Jesus, St. Peters bones, died blood of saints etc.

But that was not enough for all believers. The early church under-standing of the personal presence of the Spirit had remained even within the monolithic institution that "ruled the world." Once rediscovered, it was not again to be denied, even though it had to find its home within the church of the 14th century, not the 1st century. The effort was made to find an accommodation between the renewed realization that God's grace comes to each individual through the Holy Spirit, and the insistence of the institutional church that it alone could mediate that grace. The effort, consummated in an uneasy marriage of complete opposites, was doomed to the divorce which did occur in the Reformation. But that was to come later; and while still in the honeymoon stage, that marriage was to give birth to what was to be the next enduring phase in the church's development: Scholasticism.

Scholasticism, as if harking back to the grand design of Gnosticism to merge all religions into one unified understanding, merged theology, philosophy, science, and human reason into a unified view of magnificent and tremendous breadth. The Summa Theologiæ of Thomas Aquinas, written in the decade 1265–1274, wondrously served the institutional church, for the conclusion reached by Thomas was nothing less than total affirmation of the views of Gregory the Great, Leo III, and Innocent III. Thomas legitimatized the infallible and unrestricted sovereignty of the church over all things spiritual and secular.

As that impossible marriage was coming apart, the church had become a difficult place for clerics and bishops, even Popes, for ideas and opinions contrary to church authority were surfacing everywhere. The Gift of Aquinas was received with a thankful sigh of relief. Renewed and energized, the institution fought back against the challenges to its authority. . This is seen in the Bull of 1302, "Unum Sanctum," in which Boniface VIII put forward the claim, "It is absolutely necessary for salvation that every human creature is subject to the Roman pontiff." No Pope before him had dared to take this position, but it had to be dared now, for things had become desperate! Someone back in the first century had to be laughing, because the Trojan Horse refused by the early community, now welcomed centuries later, burst open; and as had been feared, the alien forces within poured forth fully armed for battle. And a battle it became.

When news of Boniface's pronouncement of Papal supremacy reached him, Phillip IV of France reacted with all the force and power of the newly strong, every-day-growing-stronger secular state. Phillip arranged the death of Boniface and chose his replacement in Clement V of France in 1305. Clement moved the papal court to Avignon, where it remained from 1305 to 1377, and from where seven popes ruled the church. All were French, and, it was suspected, under the undue influence of the French crown. Whether that accusation was true or not, whatever was true, the papacy in Avignon was disgracefully inadequate, failing to live up to the role of leadership in worldly affairs, which the papacy had assigned to itself, and which indeed was required if the church was to maintain its position in the world. Actually the Popes of Avignon were wholly inadequate to nearly every task; and in the absence of adequate Papal ability, one issue after another was decided by secular means and was never to be reversed.

It was the Avignon experience of the papacy which destroyed the assertion of previous Popes that secular power was subordinate to that of the Pope's and seriously undermined the competence to decide its own affairs. In September 1376, Gregory XI abandoned Avignon and moved his court to Rome, officially ending the Avignon Papacy. Or so it was thought. When Gregory died in 1378, an Italian, Urban VI, was elected Pope. The politics called the next turn! During the years in Avignon, the papal court had become well entrenched in local life and culture and the six cardinals living there wanted to remain. They feared Urban, declared his election void, and elected instead Clement VII who remained in Avignon. Urban remained in Rome, and Western Christendom had two rival Popes.

This was a sorry situation which thankfully the Council of Constance (1414 - 1418) brought to an end by deposing both Popes and declaring Martin V Pope. However, any thought that things were finally settled was premature; for just as the church took a deep sigh of relief, Martin Luther was born and things were again to be plunged into controversy. For nearly 1500 years the strong institution of the church had been able to withstand all the troubles and controversies of institutional life and remain relatively unscathed. All this was to change with Luther.

Chapter Nineteen

Reformation

Just before and during Martin Luther's lifetime, the world was rapidly changing. The medieval world was still very much present, but the seeds of a new era were everywhere. The beginning of the fifteenth century brought not only the great period of classical art--Michelangelo, Raphael, Durer, Holbein, Titan, Leonardo da Vinci and many other masters--but in 1455 Gutenberg invented the printing press; in 1485 Leonardo da Vinci invented the parachute and 10 years later excited the world with designs for a flying machine; in 1492 Columbus discovered the new world. Then in 1543 Copernicus published his bombshell that the earth is NOT the center of the universe!

Something heady was blowing in the wind, and those winds took it everywhere. Perhaps someone astute would have recalled the words of Jesus to Nicodemus that the wind of the Spirit blows where it will. The 16th century world was ripe for change; but who could ever have known that the change would split the church, leaving part as it was, and taking the other part back to the understandings of first Christian communities?

Martin Luther was born November 10, 1483, at Eisleben, Germany, the eldest of nine brothers and sisters. From the ninety-five theses nailed to the door of the Castle Church in 1517, Luther was a force for radical change in the church. Someone copied and printed the 95 theses; and the printing quickly sold out, not only in Germany, but in much of Europe. From that moment on the printing press was to be Luther's great ally, and he managed it masterfully at every opportunity. The main legacy of Luther,

Calvin, Zwingli and the other Reformers, was the returning of the New Testament to the position it had held within the young Christian community 1500 years earlier. For the 16th century reformers the New Testament was the final authority for Christian faith, not Popes and Councils which, as Luther said, demonstrably erred and in some cases connived to set doctrine to suit them and say what they desired. Far too much water had run down the river of theology for that to continue.

Luther was perhaps the first critical scholar in hundreds of years; and even as he lived in what was still a medieval world, his approach to the New Testament was more modern than medieval. To be sure, while he took a literal understanding of a Biblical text when it suited him to do so, he nonetheless taught that the New Testament must be read seriously, not literally; and as we read it, our life experience and knowledge must not be pushed aside but used to judge and understand what is being said. In this insistence Luther was smack in line with the understanding of the early church and the Gospel authors; they had done exactly that! For Luther, as for us in the 21st century, "Then is Now" all over again!

The Reformation's insistence on the ultimate authority of the New Testament did not place that authority on the fact that it had been canonized by the church, but upon the power and authority it had within the life of those who read it, as the Holy Spirit entered into that dialog. Luther said he translated the Bible into German so that his personal experience of the Holy Spirit might become available to all. He and the other Reformers taught that the certainty of salvation decided by the church at that time to be found in the power of the institution was in fact a gift of God's grace given to each person by the Holy Spirit. Certainty of salvation is found in the community of faith, they said, not in its institutional authority, but in the authority of the Gospel which it proclaims. Luther, John Calvin, Ulrich Zwingli and other Reformers were kindred spirits in realizing that the church of their time had strayed far from its origins. And then in England, in a powerful example of just how much things had changed, King Henry VIII on his own authority established the Church of England.

Now, for sure, things were no longer as they had been for the last thousand years. The institutional church was against the ropes.

But while the Church was down, it was not out. Pope Paul III (1534–1549) called the Council of Trent (1545–1563) to deal with the points raised by the Reformation. That there were corrupt priests and bishops was obvious, as was the fact that in many areas the church had simply gone too far in its use of authority. The Council agreed many abuses, particularly the use of indulgences, needed to be corrected. But the whole thrust of the Reformation, that salvation is by grace through faith alone, was rejected at this council; and it was stated that any compromise with the Protestant position on this issue or any issue was not to happen! The 1500 year history of the church, its warts and all, was reaffirmed and reasserted. In perhaps the truest sense the "Roman Catholic Church" came into being at this Council, for it asserted it alone was the true church. Then in apparent opposition to Reformation theology, it clearly stated that salvation required works as well as faith.

That assertion was not really so much a rejection of the Reformation view of salvation as it was a nuanced understanding of it. In the polemical heat of religion in that day however, much as the partisan heat of politics in our day, nuances were lost in a battle of rhetoric. The result was that from 1550 on the Western church was no longer one church, but two--Roman Catholicism and Protestantism-- with each going in its own direction. And also once again, as so many centuries earlier, it was a time of diversity in the church.

If the wind of the Spirit was behind events, the Spirit was blowing with mighty breath: Lutherans, Quakers, Methodists, Anglicans, Presbyterians, Reformed...on and on, the diversity was to continue. And, just as so many centuries before, slogans, name calling, book burning, the Inquisition and bloody wars, twisted and distorted the faith. It was an incredible, sad and sorry story, and even more was still in store.

The Reformation brought to the community another way to look at the New Testament, another view of how it should be read, and on what basis it was to be understood. Until the Reformation the church maintained that it had established the New Testament and was alone able to properly interpret it. Until the Reformation the laity was not encouraged to read the New Testament, the church fearing wide scale misunderstanding without clerical leadership. This was a more than reasonable concern. However, that leadership taught that the Bible was a divinely inspired book, written by God's intervention in such a way that it is generally inerrant and infallible and to be read literally.

Despite the Reformation imperatives not to do so, reading the New Testament literally remained the primary way to read it for many generations following the Reformation and is still popular today. This having been said, there is no single term which is exhaustively descriptive of how the New Testament has been read in the church. In the 2nd and 3rd centuries allegory was a popular, and for some of the church leaders, the preferred way in which to interpret the texts. It was obvious to them that a literal understanding resulted in too many unsupportable conclusions. Allegory removed most of those problems, and so it remained a popular method of Biblical understanding well into the middle ages.

The 16th century re-introduced the most common approach of the earliest Christian community, one that had fallen out of favor as orthodoxy combated heresy and employed literal interpretation in its defense. The Reformers were not the first to realize that a truly literal reading often led to impossible contradictions and irreconcilable difficulties and might indeed obscure the deeper and richer sub-text within what was being said. Nor were they the first to realize that on the other hand prudence said that to open the door to a non-literal understanding of the text could result in way too much room for personal views to intrude and distort, making it easy for the reader to twist the text say what the reader wanted it to say. Indeed, that did happen, and the reformers themselves arrived at very different understandings of the same text. But, prudent or not, the door was opened, and it was to remain open, and eventually, to keep the metaphor going, would be completely removed from its hinges!

The Reformation was followed by what has come to be called the Enlightenment, a period from roughly the 1650's to 1815. The

Enlightenment took the debate over how the New Testament should be read out of the hands of the church and put it into the hands of scholars and philosophers, subjecting it to the rigorous scrutiny of secular examination. "Enlightenment" is an apt word because it did indeed seem to those living then as if a veil had been removed or the shutters opened from the windows of the medieval worldview and new light and new understanding let into both the world and the church. In the heady excitement of this new self-congratulating era, real advancements in science, philosophy, politics, art, music, culture--the very fabric of society--were exploding everywhere; and to this new era, the term "dark ages" seemed to be the perfect description of the preceding period of history, which had been under control of the church.

While the Enlightenment did indeed bring a sense of freedom to philosophy, scientific, cultural, scholastic and theological disciplines, it did so with a sneering contempt for the church and the doctrines and traditions of the church. The New Testament did not escape the bright light of Enlightenment scrutiny, nor the criticism and skepticism of the eras of Reason and Romanticism, so called, which followed. By the 19th century, this resulted in a nearly complete dismantling of all previous understanding not only of how the New Testament was to be read, but whether it was to be believed in any way at all! To that story we turn next.

Chapter Twenty

Constantine von Tischendorf

The hubris of the so-called Enlightened Age and Rational Age, the centuries 1700-1900, was that human reason could comprehend and explain everything. Based upon this certainty, whatever in the New Testament did not agree with "plain reason," such as angels, miracles, visitations, resurrection appearances, or anything supernatural, was simply thrown out. The Bible no longer held a privileged status of "God given" authority; and as if a damn had broken, the view that the New Testament was no more than, no different than, any other book, flooded over the world! Yes, the New Testament was old, but rather than age giving it some patina of authority, they assumed being old meant errors, mistakes, problems of every imaginable kind had been incorporated into it. And then as if a coffin prepared for the demise of an old relic, it was asserted the New Testament was not even as old as the church claimed it was!

There was some basis for these assertions, for no manuscripts existed older than the 9th century, and there was nothing to prove it had existed before then! Of course it could be reasonably assumed the manuscripts they had were copies of earlier ones, but if applied generously, that would go back to perhaps the 6th century. This shocking trial balloon, floated tentatively at first, then became the full blown assertion that the New Testament was not written shortly after Christ's death by the apostles at all, but was the work of unknown persons in the 5th or 6th century. Merely a century earlier an idea so radical would have been dismissed out of hand as preposterous, but now it was embraced by the growing secularism of a reason centered philosophical worldview.

Of course the church had to react to this, and there were two reactions. First, the church reacted defensively, with a defiant resurgence of literal inspiration, an "in-your-face secularism, "We don't care what you say, we know the New Testament is the verbally dictated word of God. " This was unfortunate and doomed to failure. The other reaction was more positive, more productive, I believe more inspired. It was led by an amazing man, Constantine von Tischendorf, a manuscript scholar, a man of deep faith, and a man who had fantastic eyes which were to be of tremendous importance in the quest he adopted as his life's work. Tischendorf was not convinced by the secularist argument regarding the age of the New Testament, but he knew the only way to disprove it was to produce manuscripts earlier than the 9th century. Absolutely convinced in his heart that the New Testament was written by the apostles shortly after Jesus' death, he began a search that would consume the rest of his life.

About 1845 he went to the Vatican thinking something would be in the archives. He was refused access. Moving on to the Holy Land he made his way to the Monastery of St. Catherine at Mt. Sinai, in the Sinai desert, home to pious monks. The monastery had been built by order of the Emperor Justinian I (527-565) to protect the Chapel of the Burning Bush, constructed by the mother of Constantine the Great in the 300's. The chapel was to commemorate the place where Moses was given the Ten Commandments.

There are roads now, but it was an awfully inhospitable place in 1845, so remote, so hidden, you had to have good reason to go there. That fact turned out to be crucial to the success of Tischendorf's mission, because its remote location and difficult access allowed St. Catherine to escape all the ravages of history--wars, crusades, plundering and so on. Quietly and peacefully it continued in the desert for 1300 years, simply collecting and storing manuscripts. It is still the world's second largest collection of Greek manuscripts, exceeded only by the Library of the Vatican. Tischendorf introduced himself and was led by indifferent monks into an old library, stacked with scrolls--on shelves, in boxes, stuffed here and there. So many old scrolls were littered all around, he felt a sense of certainty swelling within him; this would be the place! He spent the next year at St Catherine's, sorting through manuscripts, trying to index them, bring order to them, but all he found was Old Testament, Old Testament, Old Testament. He left frustrated.

Then, in 1859, undaunted and still determined, he made one last trip to St. Catherine's. Tischendorf noticed a monk was busy packing a relic of St. Thomas to be sent to Rome. The monk was wrapping the relic in old scrolls to protect it, taking them from a large basket full of manuscripts, obviously worn and tattered, which lay at his feet. Tischendorf was certain he caught a glimpse of the words "Kata Matthew," (according to St. Matthew) on one of the pages. With an agility that belied his years he gathered up the scrolls from both the box and the basket and took them into the library. Soon loud cries of joy began to reverberate in that ancient monastery. He had found a complete New Testament! When study of the manuscript was completed, it was established it had been copied about the year 325, so the original was older still. It was an incredible find, the oldest manuscript ever. 36 pages were missing but the rest remained in excellent condition. An amazing story ...but there's more.

Ever since Tischendorf, scholars have made regular visits to the monastery; and in what is a somewhat apocrypha, somewhat accurate story, depending on which source you accept, one group of scholars witnessed a monk in the courtyard about to burn some old scrolls. They prevailed upon him to let them examine them, and they found the lost 36 pages! Whatever the actual story, if that one is not to be believed, those pages have been recovered, and thousands of manuscripts in many languages remain at the monastery, which is a source of constant discovery.

Tischendorf had proven the Bible was older than the 5th century and had completely destroyed the skeptical and self-indulgent thinking of the enlightenment-rationalism foolishness. The jewel of New Testament manuscripts that Tischendorf had found at Mt. Sinai, which he named "Sinaiticus," was a complete New Testament text. It remains not only the oldest we possess, but the gold standard by which to substantiate other manuscripts since discovered.

Then, the discovery of Sinaiticus having proven the early dating of the New Testament, the Vatican gave scholars access to a document secretly held in the archives, known as Codex Vaticanus. This manuscript had never been made available to outside scholars and was still inaccessible to them in the mid-nineteenth century when Tischendorf, like all others, had been refused access to any ancient documents. Apparently the church feared that a serious study of Codex Vaticanus might contradict in some way the official Catholic Bible, based upon the translation of St. Jerome. The discovery of Sinaiticus convinced the church it did not. Scholars were allowed access, and in 1867 Codex Testamentum Vaticanum was published for all to see.

Codex Vaticanus, dated about 350, and Codex Sinaiticus, about 325, not only do not contradict each other in any way but agree in almost every aspect of the texts; and both support the amazing accuracy of other texts which have been discovered.

As amazing as the achievement of Tischendorf and the subsequent discovery of the additional 36 pages were, a gap of about 300 years between Sinaiticus, Vaticanus, and the original texts remained. Then, in 1931, came another sensational discovery. A wealthy Christian industrialist Mr. Chester Beatty sponsored an expedition to Egypt which turned up a cache of papyrus fragments, tens of thousands of them, a whole library buried under the sand, including 11 complete manuscripts of the Old Testament and dozens of the New Testament. Named in his honor, the "Chester Beatty Papyri" are of incomparable value, much older than either Sinaiticus or Vaticanus! Because there are so many papyri, scholars have given them numbers to identify them. An example...

No. 45 contains all 4 Gospels, copied about 250
No. 46 contains all the Epistles, copied also around 250

No. 47 the Book of Revelation, copied in 290
No. 52 is a fragment of the Gospel of John, dated to about
100-150

How can these manuscripts be dated so precisely? The year was not written in the upper right hand corner, but just as there is a science to archeology in which accurate dating can be made by types and styles of pottery, so there is a science and history to handwriting and to the materials used in writing. Known as Paleography, this science studies hundreds of thousands of documents, from Scripture to shopping lists, and is able to date when a manuscript was written within a ten to twenty year period. In a sense, just as hemlines go up and down, just as we can recognize 1970's dress or 1940's hair styles, so also in those pre-printing days, there were different styles of handwriting. All small letters called Minuscule, all large letters called Uncials, a mix of both, whether the text slants right, slants left, all contribute to what is really rather accurate dating. And in addition when comparison is made with literally thousands of documents which are KNOWN to come from a certain year, there is additional assurance the text of papyri date from that same period.

Papyri No. 45 is proof that in the year 250 the Gospels of Matthew, Mark, Luke and John were in circulation in the church. No. 52 is proof that John existed before 150! And the Chester Beatty papyri are not originals, but copies, so the originals were written still earlier. Then still other discoveries began to turn up. A second century sermon which extensively quoted from all four Gospels was found, further establishing the existence of the Gospels in the early second century.

Just when you think there cannot possibly be any more revelations, the Bodmer family in Geneva Switzerland, wealthy bankers for centuries, who maintained castles in various parts of Europe, did an inventory of the family assets. In a 4th floor storeroom of their castle in Basel, Switzerland curators found a complete Gospel of John, a large portion of Luke, and complete copies of 1st and 2nd Peter. In better than legible shape, the documents were very probably from 100 -125.

Currently there are thousands of complete or fragmented Greek and Latin New Testament manuscripts, and additional thousands in other languages, including Syrian, Slavic, Gothic, Ethiopic, Coptic and Armenian. There is no longer any question of the authenticity of the New Testament.

While the manuscript discoveries established the first century creation of the Gospels and Epistles, their discovery also opened the door to far more critical study of the texts. The Epistles or letters present few problems for scholars because they were directly written by the author; there was no period of oral transmission. The Gospels, however, present a different set of problems, for as we have noted, there was a period of 20-30 years of oral remembrance before they were written down. This immediately questioned the accuracy of remembrance after that period of time and birthed a great effort called historical-critical study. So named, it is an attempt to peel away probable errors or mistakes of remembrance, or of copyists, hoping to discover the actual words Jesus said not what the Gospel authors remembered, or perhaps surmised he had said. We look more carefully at this "Quest" next.

Chapter Twenty-One

Quest for the Historical Jesus

It was the 19th and 20th centuries which brought into being what came to be called the "historical-critical method" of reading the New Testament, which remains the dominant approach to Biblical criticism among scholars today. Scholars of that era were certain that human reason was capable of both comprehending and explaining everything, and equally certain that scientific principles could become the method for properly reading the New Testament. The intent of what came to be called "The Search for the Historical Jesus," or "The Quest for the Historical Jesus," was to "peel off" the layers of legend and myth it was assumed must have accumulated over the years and "get back" to the actual words of Jesus.

A worthy goal, but it was doomed to fail because Mark, Matthew, Luke and John did not write biography; they wrote apologetics, which is the theological term for the defense of a point of view. They wrote, as John put it, "So that you might believe," selecting and adapting the tradition and remembrances of the community to convince others of its truth. As it dawned upon those 19th century scholars that the Gospel writers were not biographers, they determined to study them in the same way other authors are studied and applied to the New Testament what they considered to be scientific tools which could be used for the critical study of any type of literature.

The first tool is called **Source Criticism**, by which is meant the attempt to determine possible sources for the Gospels in addition to the oral stories that were thought to lie behind the Gospels. For example, if the Gospel author was John the disciple, or if Mark was indeed a follower of Jesus and not only a companion of Peter in Rome, those would be eye witness accounts additional to the oral traditions of the early community. It worked; it was Source Criticism which determined that Mark was the first Gospel written when a study of Matthew and Luke showed that they extensively copied from Mark, meaning Mark had to have existed first. And when Luke says he wrote his Gospel after "many have already done this," how many is many? Did he mean only Mark and Matthew, or maybe also John, or the "alternative gospels" from Nag Hammadi? Some of those date from before Luke and could have been used by him, in fact may have been used by Mark and John as well. Source criticism explores all available documents to see if, or in what way, they impact the four Gospels we have.

The second tool, **Literary Criticism,** is concerned with the finished product, which we have as a Gospel or letter, and attempts to determine when it was written, who the author was, what audience the author was writing for, and his reason or purpose in writing. Literary criticism has helped a great deal in discovering insertions into the text that were not originally there. It exposes language, style, syntax etc. in the insertion that is unlike the main body of the text.

The third tool, **Form Criticism,** is based upon the assumption that the oral tradition is the first and most important of the sources for the Gospels, and although not likely the verbatim words of Jesus, best represents the essence of what Jesus said and did. The study of how oral traditions are remembered and preserved soon showed that invariably something akin to paraphrase crept in; and what actually happened, what Jesus actually said or did, became somewhat adjusted. But many of the true original words of Jesus were also preserved, and form criticism tries to identify them. While the most subjective of the critical tools, and the most uncertain, form criticism is a valuable tool for understanding the New Testament.

The last tool we will mention, **Redaction Criticism,** assumes the meaning of those parables, or miracles, or liturgies which the author included in his Gospel, can be understood only when we know the viewpoint of the writer and of the community for whom he was writing--why the stories were told in the manner they were and why some stories or sayings were chosen and others were not. Perhaps the most important contribution of redaction criticism is that it emphasizes the creative and editorial role the writers had in the production of their Gospel, as well as the realization that they had a theological purpose in writing and a target audience in mind, all of which influenced the ultimate gospel produced.

These tools were quite subjective, for it was almost inevitable that the personal bias and opinion of the scholar making the determination would influence the conclusion that was reached. While "The Quest for the Historical Jesus," ultimately failed, it did produce wondrous fruit, very tasty and fresh, which still nourishes scholars in both the Protestant and Catholic Church today. Perhaps the most important benefit was to set in place the order in which the Gospels were written and to provide a generally accepted set of dates for their composition. We are grateful to those scholars for the many doors they opened to New Testament understanding, especially the door to an open mind, which alone enables openness to the Holy Spirit, who will come, and who, as St. John put it, "...guides us into all truth..."

Chapter Twenty-Two

Results of the Quest

The legacy of the Quest for the Historical Jesus, while neither all good nor all bad, did result by the middle of the 20th century in a very sterile New Testament, lacking the passion and burning zeal that had so characterized the early Christian community, none of whom would likely recognize what those scholars had produced!

But the wind of the Spirit was still blowing, and into that unfortunate situation came a professor of theology and parish pastor in the Reformed/ Lutheran tradition, Karl Barth (1886-1968). He argued in the 1920's for a richer and fuller method to be applied to New Testament criticism. While continuing to accept the historical-critical method as a scholarly means to understand the Biblical texts, he insisted the authority of the New Testament was unique and divine; it was more than simply a book among other books and could not be read as other literature was read.

Barth's correction renewed enthusiasm for what had become a colorless and deadly boring Scripture. He insisted the original intent of the New Testament authors was to speak God's word to reader and believer in a way that was relevant to his or her personal life. The New Testament is not merely a collection of old writings to be honored, but a living document which is used by the Holy Spirit to speak God's word to the Christian community. This truth had been almost completely lost.

Then, in strong agreement with Barth, a fellow professor, Rudolf Bultmann, (1884-1976) took Barth's insight to a deeper and ultimately far more radical position. Bultmann attempted to utilize the worldview of the increasingly secular 20th century as the means to understand the New Testament in the "modern era." He concluded that, since it is human experience that miracles do not happen, the miracles in the New Testament did not happen. Those miracles, he said, are not physically real events but "myths" which attempt to explain events unexplainable in any other way. Right on, Pastor Bultmann-- myth is a literary method of the early church to capture a truth which could not be expressed in any other way. The thrust of this book is that all myth is basically metaphor; Bultmann, to be fair to him, did not make the equation between the two as being identical. I do. Myth is metaphor.

Not for that reason alone, but from that point on, Dr. Bultmann and I part ways. We agree that Easter was an event which broke the boundaries of human experience up to that time and surpasses human ability to understand in a literal manner. However, Bultmann then says the myth of Easter must be recast into a form more relevant to the way in which modern hearers of the New Testament understand reality. The Resurrection and all New Testament miracles must be "demythologized." Since we no longer think in terms of myth and poetry, metaphor and simile, we must recast those images into current worldview terms of expression, better suited for modern readers.

During the 1950's and 60's those ideas of Bultmann were taken beyond his intentions by those who also sought to make the faith "relevant" to the sensibilities of "modern humans." I will not go into all the permutations of theological imagination which ensued except to say that the result of all this well-intentioned effort was to create distortion and confusion that otherwise would not have occurred. It's like salt in food; a little bit improves the taste, but too much, and the food is unpalatable. And no one will bother with unpalatable food. Therefore comes the question, how are we to read the New Testament? That question moves us into the heart of this little book.

Here we are, in the beginning of the 21st century, having inherited a long history of New Testament interpretation which has swung like a pendulum back and forth, and then as if something snapped began erratically twirling about before crashing to the floor in pieces. "In pieces" does seem to be where New Testament understanding is at today, and like Humpty Dumpty, it cannot be put back together again. In the 21st century the question in the mind of everyone is; what is the New Testament saying to me? In what way is the Spirit speaking to me in this? Luther, Barth and Bultmann, and (contemporary Roman Catholic scholars, Hans Kung and Edward Schillebeeckx among others), would be pleased, for they would say that IS the right question to ask.

Yes, it is. But when we ask that question, how do we guard against simply creating our own meaning for the text? The danger of finding in the New Testament support for a particular agenda is seen in the efforts to interpret the New Testament from a Marxist viewpoint, a feminist viewpoint, a "gay'" viewpoint, an African-American viewpoint, a liberation viewpoint--all of which have been done in recent decades. The New Testament would neither have endured as long as it has, nor could it endure long into the future, if unfettered personal interpretation were the normal and reasonable way to read it.

On the other hand, a totally objective text that means just what it says and can be understood in only one definitive way does not exist either. This is a fortunate thing, for if such a version did exist, then there would be no personal relevance to the New Testament at all! No personal involvement can be had with a virginal text that forbids any intercourse with the reader or hearer but simply exists, high on a pedestal, to be worshiped but never appropriated as one's own.

Now all of that brings us to the assumption of this book; that what the New Testament meant to those who read it 2000 years ago is also what it means to us today. There is no qualitative difference in what it meant then and what it means now; and so for us today the right way to read the New Testament is to assume, "Then is Now!" Therefore, in disagreement with the need for demythologizing the New Testament, I say that our modern world is not that uniquely different from our forebears in any essential human manner. Around the campfire 2000 years ago they asked the same questions we continue to ask today: "Who am I? Why am I?' What is this life all about?" "Does it end when I die?" Although universally asked, none of these questions are seeking an objective answer, a philosophical answer or a scientific answer; all are personal in intent and desire; we want to know what the answer is "for me."

That is the right question, for the answer of the New Testament is always to tell us that it means we are loved by God...we are loved by God....we are loved by God. It is the loud and insistent cry of both the Old Testament and the New Testament that we are God's chosen people, called into relationship with God in the fellowship of faith in which we share with one another the love, grace, and forgiveness God gives to each one of us in the Lord Jesus Christ. So, yes, the answer of the New Testament to the questions of life is a personal answer; but that answer is given and comes alive for us only within the community of faith, in which it always directs us towards others, always demands action within the community and out from the community into the world. By community of faith is meant all versions and varieties of the Christian family --Protestant, Roman Catholic, and Greek Orthodox.

In Part four we will look at two examples of how to read the New Testament in the 21st century by taking two of the most crucial assertions, derided and ridiculed by many as being impossible to believe: the birth of Jesus and the resurrection of Jesus. We will see that, when we read them as they were intended to be read, not as myths to de-mythologize for modern sensibilities but as myths and metaphors to be understood as myths and metaphors, they recover the passion and excitement they held for that first community of believers.

Part Four

The Birth Narratives

Chapter Twenty-Three

21ˢᵗ Century Worldview

In this part we examine the New Testament narratives about the birth, death, and resurrection of Jesus. Looking at these three narratives is the best way to illustrate that the Bible must be taken seriously but not literally, and must be read within the worldview and culture of its time. "Worldview" is a term often used to describe the implicit understandings we have about the world around us. The culture of every generation is a view of the world that is built from within and is based upon an understanding of how the world works, where it came from, what it means, and what place we human beings have in it. Worldviews are not static but are constantly changing.

In Part Two we covered how new discoveries usher in a new worldview. Copernicus, Columbus, E=mc2, Charles Darwin, the Big Bang theory, all were events of sufficient magnitude they changed the worldview which existed at the time of their discovery. The terrorist attack on the World Trade Center on September 11, 2001 is perhaps such an event, for it changed life in the United States in profound ways which are still playing out in the politics, immigration policy, and other social aspects of United States culture. Usually our worldview is simply absorbed from our culture. Family, school, church, the community and country in which we live all share in a common understanding, and each reinforces the other to present a cohesive way of looking at life which is unconsciously assumed to be true.

Occasionally we question the worldview of things we were given from past generations. Sometimes we reject it or modify it because it doesn't seem to fit the facts as we encounter them. But most of the time it is hard to break out of the worldview of our time and place, hard to think out of the box, so to speak. And, to be sure, there is great power in the views in which we were raised. How life was explained to us as children, the reasons given for why we did various everyday things, gave us a secure place within the progression of human history. We accepted these explanations as truth, and they became the way in which we regarded and understood the world.

As a child grows, new experiences, education, social involvement, and perhaps exposure to other cultures and views can be a very jarring experience, requiring changes to what he or she thought was a complete and adequate understanding of reality. So disrupting can this be that some reject it and simply deny that it is true. It is almost impossibly difficult to think outside the culture in which we were raised. This was true for the writers of the New Testament as well.

It is foolish for us to assume the Gospel authors anticipated the rise of nationalism in the 18th century, Einstein in the 20th, or any contemporary world situation. It is equally foolish to think they were somehow isolated from the time and place in which they lived. No, they were fully a part of the everyday life of their times. This means that, as the authors of the Gospels and Letters wrote down the events they had witnessed, inevitably their stories and remembrances were written from within the scientific and cultural viewpoints, the prejudices and attitudes, the worldview of the time in which they lived. It could be no other way.

For example, we may wish the New Testament were not so sexist in its language, but it is because it was a patriarchal, male-dominated culture. Women held a secondary position in society and were dependent upon husbands and male children for their livelihood and their very survival. In most parts of the world today we no longer hold those attitudes, but they were the culture of that time. We may also wish the New Testament didn't speak about heaven above and hell below, Jesus ascending into the clouds, the sun standing still, and other images from an ancient worldview, but those images and expressions were part of the culture, the way things were expressed at that time. The New Testament was written to be read by people who would clearly understand the images being used. We no longer share that worldview, and in order for those images and metaphors to make sense to us, we need to realize they ARE metaphors and not literal statements.

Sometimes we also need to make simple adjustments to accommodate the culture of that time, such as when only men are mentioned or the masculine gender is used exclusively. It was never the intention of the writer to exclude women; they simply understood in that culture that women **were** included, an assumption that remained until recent generations. The easy fix to this can be taken care of in translation; simply change 5000 men to read 5000 men and women, or change brothers in Christ to read brothers and sisters in Christ. That would be a correct reading of the writer's intention and would not change the intention or meaning of what is being said. That is being done.

Some things though are not so easily changed and require a reinterpretation of what is being said. The ascension of Jesus, as Luke records it in the book of Acts, for example, while a metaphoric expression for Jesus returning to the place where God is, is also something which could be said to make reasonable sense in the first century when the world view of the day envisioned a three tiered existence; heaven above, hell below, earth in the middle. So, when Jesus returned to God, where else would he go, but "above?" The understanding of the day was a flat world. It was thought to be quite possible to build a tower to heaven or for a ladder to come down from heaven and angels use it to move up and down. But it must still be emphasized that this whole understanding was never thought to be literally true. It was always more of a spiritual or mythological realization, a way of affirming that there is more to life than we can see. And they knew well from their experience what we too have learned from ours--that some things cannot be easily represented by words, but require images and imagination.

The first century also believed in demon possession and unclean spirits as being the cause of some illnesses. It is the hubris of the 21st century to dismiss such ideas as superstition or naiveté, even though the presence of the evil and the demonic can truly be seen in our present world by those who have the eyes to see it. While in our worldview we go to an M.D., not an exorcist, the more we learn about the causes of some illness and disease, the more evil abounds and twisted ideologies proliferate, the less we can so easily dismiss the idea of demons and spirits and evil forces in the universe! On November 11, 2014, the United States Conference of Catholic Bishops approved a new Rite of Exorcism, thus bringing demons and possession back into serious discussion.

To be sure to some extent, the New Testament can be read literally or as allegory, yet the deepest truth, as we know well enough, cannot always be expressed adequately in words. Sometimes the best way will be a metaphor. Sometimes an allegory may be correct. And sometimes, the text does indeed mean what it says in a literal sense. So when we read the New Testament what is required of us is to enter into a dialog with it, seek to understand the intention, not only the words themselves. That is not always easy, but we will try to do that next, as we look at some of the metaphorical images of the New Testament which try to capture or understand the incredible event that happened among them in the resurrection of Jesus from the dead.

The incredible delight of a crisp fresh apple picked off the tree is perhaps indescribable, but it is a wondrous experience. The early community had wondrous experiences of the risen Jesus, incredible experiences of the Holy Spirit in their lives, miracles and unexplainable flights of wondrous peace and certainty filled their spirits. They knew what they knew because they could not deny they had experienced it, and they tried with everything in their power to tell us about it. So we will look at what the New Testament tells us about the experiences of the first Christian community by opening our hearts and minds and letting the Spirit lead us, as they intended we would do.

Chapter Twenty-Four

Faith like a Child

Jesus said, "Unless you have faith like a little child…," you will not understand. He was perhaps speaking primarily about the open-mindedness of children and their ability to trust on the basis of relationship. Still, while it may not be the primary meaning of what Jesus was saying, it is also important to note that children are very open to mythological thinking. Imaginary friends are not uncommon, and children often experience interactions with them. However they are almost always very aware these are "pretend' friends, and not real. This shows a high level of mythological openness on the part of children to believe in the possibility of everything--dragons, fairies, princesses and heroes with great powers. Children have a faculty of mind that opens them to a world much greater than what their five senses tell them. And they are the wiser for that!

But we lose that ability as we age. Why? We become realists, or so we think. Actually this loss of open-minded possibility is the consequence of 400 years of so-called scientific thinking. The material realism of the 19th and early 20th centuries is still very much with us, insisting that only what you can see and touch is real. Therefore, since you can not touch them, mystical experiences, miracles and spiritual realities are merely constructs of the mind, without any reality outside the individual's own consciousness. That, many maintain, is the scientific truth. Well, not really. Most definitely not entirely, for there is ample equally scientific evidence which validates every one of those "constructs" of the mind. As Hamlet said, "There are more things in heaven and earth, Horatio, than are dreamt of in your philosophy" (Hamlet (1.5.167-8); and in the 21st century we see the truth of that on an almost daily basis!

Classical physics, the mother of "material realism," is somewhat on the ropes today, as quantum physics speaks of miracles and spiritual experiences as phenomenon which does not violate the rules or laws of physics and are not only possible, but probable, occurrences. By golly, that's exactly what they understood back in the first century! We are not, as we like to think, smarter, more enlightened and sophisticated than that earlier generation. In fact, we are in many ways poorer and lesser than they for having lost the ability to think in a metaphorical and spiritual manner. Oh, to be a child again!

It has been the gold standard during the last three centuries of New Testament criticism to relegate metaphor and mythological thinking to a marginal place and, as Sergeant Friday put it, get "the facts, only the facts." (Jack Webb of the television series Dragnet) The 18th-20th centuries wanted only the facts because the Biblical criticism of that era was built upon what they thought were the true insights of material realism. They were certain the earlier centuries were primitive and childlike, and the metaphors and myths of that day, not being real, were badly in need of being demythologized for more critical thinking.

Well, yes, and yet not so much, yes. In reading the New Testament we must employ both critical thinking and mythological thinking. Critical thinking means not to take something at what it says alone but to look for what it intends to say. To do this takes the eyes of a little child. A child has no difficulty in holding two somewhat opposing concepts at the same time. He or she does not doubt that both can be equally true. In physics and philosophy, and in theology, this is called "complementarity." And, far from being merely a childish point of view, it is absolutely necessary in order to understand reality as it is being increasingly understood in modern physics and to help us disengage from a literal interpretation of the New Testament. If we take Jesus' resurrection, his transfiguration, his ascension literally, none of those images make sense to the contemporary mind; and since in our sophistication we immediately smile at the foolishness of believing such things actually happened, we miss what that image is really saying. It cannot get through to us. But when we apply critical thinking, we say, since this is obviously not literally true, something more is being told here and we need to get behind the surface of the story. We must look behind or within what is being said to get at what is really being said, and that requires the metaphorical, mythological thinking of a little child. Perhaps that is why Jesus said, *"Truly, I tell you, whoever does not receive the kingdom of God as a little child will never enter it."* (Luke 18:17)

The modern mind, or whatever we might term the current viewpoint, is not the measure of truth and all things. The writers of the New Testament were ignorant of 21st century modes of thinking, but they were not ignorant people. They used myth and metaphor in expressing the spiritual experiences in their lives, because in the end it is the only way to really get at what they wanted to say. To think mythologically is to see with the eyes of a little child which understands all things are possible. It is to have, as Jesus put it, "...eyes that see ...ears that hear," (Mark 8:18). This is not impossible for us to do, for in contemporary cosmological thinking and quantum physics, some of the things that the physicists and astronomers are describing are downright magical and incredible. And yet those things are the ground floor of physics today; and to really be a 21st century person, mystical, mythological thinking is a necessity. So, when reading the New Testament we must let myths be myths, metaphors remain metaphors, and understand both for what they are. Not to do this, and to instead take them literally or to try to demythologize them, turns the stories into sterile accounts which say nothing of much substance, because all the wonder, the joy, the incredible newness of what they are describing is lost.

For example, it is said that a picture is worth a thousand words. That says it clearly....words are sometimes inadequate to express the experience of a sunset, or the first kiss, or falling in love. But, if all we have with which to express those amazing experiences are words, then what must we do? Paint a word picture! And this is best done with images. "An angel visited." Does that not stir the imagination? "The devil took Jesus to a high mountain." Is that not a powerful and evocative image? The New Testament is filled with stories which are really word pictures. Jesus was a master at telling stories, and his parables resonate with everyone who hears them even 2000 years after the telling, because they capture in words what can only be captured in words that are really word pictures... the image of a father, a king, a man sowing seeds.

Let me give a small example of how a word picture captures so much more than mere words alone. This comes from Carl Sandberg ...Chicago Poems, 1916:

> The fog comes
> on little cat feet.
> It sits looking
> over harbor and city
> on silent haunches
> And then moves on.

That's a metaphoric image and a great one. The Biblical writers are equally as gifted, and they give us images and metaphors which capture what a literal description could never do. They put the mystery of what is happening in the events of Jesus' ministry into images that make that mystery understandable. The intention of the New Testament is not to give us history, even though it is written in that form. It is not to give us a biography of Jesus, although it is the form into which the substance of Jesus' ministry is put. But actually that is merely the package or wrapper for the gift inside. You don't eat the banana skin; you eat the fruit inside it. When we read the Holy Scriptures we are dealing with spiritual realities and experiences of the early community which we cannot understand any more than we understand the spiritual experiences and miracles of our own lives.

That difficulty in understanding spiritual things is very well described for us in John's story of Nicodemus. Nicodemus comes to Jesus seeking spiritual insight. Jesus tells him he must be born again. Nicodemus takes him literally, not metaphorically, and asks, "How can I reenter the womb and be born again?" That is precisely where literal reading will take you... into foolishness. Jesus patiently tells Nicodemus, "What I am saying is that you must be born of the spirit." All believers have this spiritual sense of having been born again by the Holy Spirit. And Jesus is saying the agency of the Holy Spirit accomplishes this within our present being and existence. We do not re-enter the womb but neither are we lifted out of ourselves into some heavenly sphere. God comes to us in the physical condition in which we exist and redeems and reshapes our existence by incorporating us into the reality that is his Son Jesus. (John 3: 1-21)

We are flesh and blood, and in the incarnation of Jesus, God too becomes flesh and blood. God doesn't take us out of ourselves into his realm but he enters into ours. In doing this he validates our physical existence as being not a lesser form of existence, but one worthy of God's concern and involvement. And even though the flesh and blood Jesus has a genealogy the same as we do, as Luke and Matthew carefully remind us, he is neither determined nor limited by his genealogy. And Jesus says to Nicodemus, and to us, neither are you! We are more than we appear to be, for in Jesus' resurrection we too are reborn from above. Our flesh and blood conception and birth would limit us to an existence in the physical realm, but they no longer define the whole of who we are. Reborn in the Spirit, we are more than flesh and blood alone. The reality of who we are has changed completely even though our outward appearance remains the same.

Our true relationship with Jesus is not only one of sharing blood and flesh but of also sharing the spirit of God within us. As St. Paul tells us, when the Holy Spirit brings us into union with Christ, when we are in Christ, and he is in us, then we, as He is, are also in God. (Romans 7:4) What this is saying is that we need to take the humanity of our Lord with utter seriousness. Jesus was true man, fully and completely human, with no outward sign or evidence of his heavenly parentage. We have noted how the Gospels presented this quite clearly. This is a crucial fact to keep in mind as we look at the virgin birth of Jesus in the next chapter.

But before we turn to that, just think for a minute about birth itself, your birth, everyone's birth. Who could, even for a moment, consider human birth to be merely a physical event? Is it not way too mysterious to think that? It is a physical event of course, but whom of us has not held the newborn child in our hands and been overwhelmed by the mystery of a new being coming into our world! Overcome by the unknown possibilities we hold in our hands, and by the awesome responsibility which requires of us unconditional commitment, and trust in ourselves and in our child as we guide this little biological phenomenon through the inevitabilities of growth, childhood, adolescence! Do we not call the birth of our child a miracle? And is it not truly a miracle? By this do we mean it is a miraculous birth? Well, yes, in a sense we do, for are we not saying it is a birth like that of Jesus, who, remember is a human being in every way as we are. Does "in every way" include his birth?

To be sure we say Jesus was "conceived of the Holy Spirit." But is that also true of all who are born again in Christ? I think yes, and when John tells us of the incarnation of Jesus, rather than telling a birth story, John says "and the Word became flesh and lived among us..." (John 1:14) In exactly what manner that happened does not concern John. Nor, as we will see did it interest Mark. Then John goes on to add a most significant addendum to Jesus birth: *"But to all who received him, who believed in his name, he gave power to become children of God, who were born, not of blood or of the will of the flesh or of the will of man, but of God."* (John 1: 12, 13) So is Jesus the son of God in the same way we are? Or is Jesus truly the 'one who came down from Heaven"? That's the question for the next Chapter.

Chapter Twenty-Five

Introduction to the Virgin Birth

The concept of a virgin birth for Jesus is barely mentioned in the New Testament. Mark, John and Paul never mention Jesus' birth at all. It is Matthew and Luke who introduce Jesus' birth, and we will look at that after a brief look at what Mark, John and Paul do have to say.

Mark

Mark's omission of Jesus' birth is striking. Quite the opposite of the miraculous conception and birth we will find in Matthew and Luke, in Mark Jesus' birth and early life was so common and ordinary there was no need to mention it. In fact its very normalcy raised doubts when he begins to claim who he is. As Jesus preaches in Nazareth, his neighbors said, "Is this not the boy who used to deliver our newspapers? "

Actually they said, 'Is not this the carpenter, the son of Mary, the brother of James and Joses and Jude and Simon? And are not his sisters here with us?' And they were offended by him." (6:3) Jesus responds to them, "A prophet has no honor in his own country and among his own kin and house." (Mark 6:4) In Mark's opinion nothing of unusual significance or even particular interest took place in Jesus' life until his baptism, when Jesus accepts his ministry and God declares who he really is; "You are my Son, the Beloved; with you I am well pleased." (1:11) Remember in Mark's version of Jesus baptism, God speaks only to Jesus, so typical for Mark; there is no objective indication of a super-natural relationship to God. It was up to Matthew and Luke to add that concept to Jesus' life and ministry.

John

For John the whole idea of a virginal conception was irrelevant. It was the event of the resurrection that so impressed itself upon John he can hardly think of anything else as mattering at all! The overriding concern of John, the only question of importance to him, is whether when the Holy Spirit brings us to the moment of God's grace in Jesus, we accept it or reject it. That's all John cares about. He has no interest in anything which has as its goal an outward or objective proof that Jesus is divine, and he stresses the ordinary human situation of Jesus, who looks and seems just like everybody else. In truth Jesus **is** more than he seems, but the ability to know that is something which must be given by the Holy Spirit.

Paul.

We must also consider St. Paul, whose letters to the churches, as best we know, pre-date all of the Gospels. Paul does not make any comment on Jesus' virgin birth. The perfect opportunity for him to have done that is the beginning of Romans. Paul is speaking to a largely Jewish-Christian community, and they would have been excited to hear it if Paul had made the connection to the prophecy of Isaiah that "A virgin shall conceive." But he doesn't. What Paul does do is to say, "The Gospel concerning God's son, who was descended from David according to the flesh and designated Son of God by his resurrection from the dead." (1:4) Take note that Paul says God's validation of Jesus comes not in his birth, but in his resurrection.

Then his letter to the Galatians provided another perfect opportunity for Paul to refer to a virgin birth for Jesus, but again he does not. He says, "...but when the time had fully come God sent forth his son, born of a woman, born under the law to redeem those who were under the law ..." (4:4) Born of a woman, not a virgin. Paul insists Jesus is fully one of us in all ways, including his birth. Since it is a birth like ours that makes Jesus one with us, a supernatural birth would drive a wedge into that whole reality; actually it would destroy the solidarity completely, and lead to what it indeed does to lead to, the whole supernatural emphasis placed upon Jesus' ministry in the later Gospels of Matthew and Luke.

In contrast to what we will see in Matthew and Luke, Mark, John and Paul tell us Jesus was in every discernable way as ordinary as everyone else. This was just fine for the early community, for they had known Jesus, and many had experienced the resurrected Jesus or were personally involved with those who had. All of this changed as new members came into the churches, who did not have personal acquaintance with Jesus but whom, as Jesus said to Thomas, were asked to believe without seeing. For them, as Einstein said was true for him, a picture was worth a thousand words.

It is the genius of Matthew and Luke that they provided pictures, images, stories, presented in a wondrous mixture of myth, metaphor, and glorious imagination. A literary method never intended to be taken literally, Biblical myth is a way of saying that a spiritual experience happened; and it was a real experience, not an imagined one. It may have come in a dream, which is not necessarily merely a dream, but as psychology and physics are teaching us, can be an experience of something that is real in another dimension of reality.

We need a short detour here, because ever since the enlightenment and the rationalism of the 17th and 18th centuries, we have been told that there are two realities which are mutually exclusive. That is, the inner world of human consciousness and the outer world of physical reality, which are separated by an abyss that cannot be bridged. The theological view of the first century denies this. And so does the quantum physics of the 21st century, which has demolished both that abyss and the two realities idea. In its place it asserts the strong possibility that spiritual experiences are as real as every other experience. For many this is a striking assertion, because so far only the most courageous of empirical scientists have been willing to speak out about the findings which do support paranormal abilities like extrasensory perception, near death experiences, and the like. The majority of scientists today continue to reject belief in anything transcendent. They are good classical material realists. As a result, there is great social pressure among scientists to reduce all scientific explanations to material mechanisms, and to reject consideration of any phenomena that cannot be explained by those materialistic mechanisms.

Well, the New Testament Gospels beg to differ with them. Mythological language is good modern physics. Good science. Good theology. On the one hand, a dream may be equally as substantial and real an experience as a physical one. On the other hand, it may be the only way really possible to express a visitation of the Spirit which usually exceeds words to describe it. On either hand it cannot be dismissed "out of hand." (Oh my, pardon that, I couldn't resist!)

We have all had spiritual experiences, and while we find it difficult to put into words, we know it was a real experience. This was equally true for the first century, which knew more about reality than we have been willing to give them credit for knowing. To see how this works in the Gospel nativity narratives, we turn to Matthew first, then Luke. Unfortunately, in general awareness, Matthew's stories have been merged together with Luke's into one narrative; and over the years the stories have been so mingled together in Christmas pageants and worship readings, that few of us, without sitting down and carefully studying it, could say whether the Roman tax census is reported in Luke or in Matthew, or which of them includes the circumcision or Herod's crafty consultation with the Magi.

The various episodes of the Christmas story are woven together in our minds and the minds of our children, who with the wisdom of youthful insight have no problem with adding Santa Claus, reindeers, Christmas trees, Frosty, and so forth to the Nativity story. Children are wonderful. Can we become one for a little while? Put on your childlike faith, and walk with me through some beautiful stories about miracles and wonders beyond the knowing. We are thankful to Matthew and Luke for giving them to us! So let's look next at their story.

Chapter Twenty-Six

Birth of Jesus in Matthew

As we look at the accounts of Jesus' birth, Matthew comes first. He was writing for the Jews who were converting and those who were interested in Jesus but not sure enough to make a decision. For them Matthew wants to place Jesus' birth within the larger picture of God's long plan of the ages to bring about the day of the Messiah. The coming of the Messiah had been long prophesized in the Hebrew Scriptures, and many expectations had built up. The Messiah would have to fulfill these to be accepted. Matthew intends to show, even if it is a stretch once in a while, that the birth of Jesus fulfilled every prophecy and expectation regarding the Messiah in the Hebrew Scriptures.

In the popular opinion of that time, the most essential of those conditions, although somewhat confusing and contradictory, were that Jesus be the Son of David, that he come from Bethlehem, that he was called out of Egypt, and that he is a Nazarene. Matthew's birth narrative includes all of those expectations as he attempts to convince those Jews who are open to being convinced that Jesus is the promised Messiah. I have a great respect for this tradition, held in faith by generations, and wholeheartedly agree with Matthew's intention and the narrative he wove to present it. It's a beautiful story and I would not want to do without it.

Matthew goes about his task very carefully. He had to provide Jesus with a proper pedigree as a descendant of David, so he includes a genealogy, which shows he is a descendant of Abraham and a member of the Royal House of David, and therefore able to claim he is the son of David. (1:1-17) Just as Matthew had cleverly divided his Gospel into 5 chapters to replicate the Torah, so also he divides the genealogy into 3 groups of 14 generations each.

The first group of 14 begins with Abraham and ends with Jesse. The second group of 14 begins with David and ends with Jechoniah, the last king of Judah who was carted off to Babylon by Nebuchadnezzar. The third group ends with Matthew's purpose in presenting the genealogy: "Joseph, the husband of Mary, of whom Jesus was born, who is called the Messiah."

You perhaps notice the problem here. While Joseph was indeed of the House of David, Mary was not, and it presents a difficult chore for Matthew to claim Jesus as a descendant of David, but also claim the birth of Mary's child was a birth in which Joseph had no part. His whole genealogy is somewhat curious because in Judaism lineage is traced through the mother not the father, so Matthew's attempt to trace Jesus' genealogy through the father's side is very unusual. However, as Matthew continues he slips a number of times and says Joseph was Jesus' father.

Now it could be that there is another reason which made it a necessity for Matthew to record Jesus' genealogy. Some of the Jews were accusing Jesus of being illegitimate, "At least we are not born of fornication." (John 8:41) The Talmud, a commentary on the Jewish Scriptures, which was considered to have equal weight and validity to Scripture, rather slanderously claims that Jesus was the bastard son of a Roman soldier named Panterus who seduced Mary. There is no evidence for this and no mention of Jesus' illegitimacy anywhere else in the New Testament. So possibly it was a slur said in a moment of frustration. But it could be that clever Matthew, writing for Jews who would have been familiar with that comment, decides to take the accusation head on. I think this is his plan because he includes in his genealogy five women, three of whom were ancestresses of King David.

The first, Tamer, seduced her father-in-law; the second Rahab, was a prostitute in Jericho; the third is Ruth, who has nothing questionable about her character, except she was a Moabite, not a Jew. And yet that "except" is somewhat of a problem, because Ruth, a Moabite, not a Jew, is the great grandmother of David! Finally, as perhaps the last and best, Matthew brings in Bathsheba, the wife of Uriah, mother of Solomon, who was conceived in an affair with David, and thus is also a less than sterling example of purity as well. So we see that all the women in the Messianic genealogy were very open to the same criticism that was levied against Mary!

Isn't it great what Matthew does here! It's a great way to say "You who are so malicious in your comments about Mary would do well to remember the ancestresses of the great king David." How easy it is, says Matthew, to criticize when you do not discern the divine purpose that is behind Jesus' birth. God was at work in David's house and in David's descendent Jesus; God still is at work among us! The genealogy of Jesus is thus to some extent a defense of Mary against those Jews who accused Jesus of being illegitimate and a validation of her and her son for those who wanted to accept Jesus as the Messiah. The Gospel is related to life, isn't it!

Matthew's Birth Story

Moving now into the birth story itself, Matthew has only two references to it being a virgin birth. The first is Matthew's statement that, "When his mother Mary had been engaged to Joseph but before they lived together she was found to be with child from the Holy Spirit." (1:18) Mary was pregnant and Joseph was not a party to it. Matthew then tells us Joseph has a very human concern about this and a very difficult decision to make. But before he can make it, it is solved for him by the visitation of an angel in a dream. Matthew's second reference to Mary's virginity is when he quotes the prophecy in Isaiah, "Look, the young woman is with child and shall bear a son, and shall name him Immanuel..." (Isaiah 18:24)

Matthew's concern, throughout his Gospel, is to convince the Jews that Jesus does fulfill all the prophecies of the Messiah. So Matthew says he is born of the house of David, he is Emmanuel, he comes from Bethlehem, he is called out of Egypt, and he is a Nazarene. So far, up to that point, all of the prophecy of Isaiah is fulfilled, except only that in the Septuagint translation of Isaiah he had prophesied the Messiah would be born of a virgin. Matthew must make that connection as well. It would be frosting to the argument. Except, the recipe for the frosting is unclear! There is a linguistic confusion in this prophecy of Isaiah which came about in a very common way. Many Jews had moved from Palestine into other parts of the empire, adopted the Gentile culture and spoke Greek, the cultured language of the day. Primarily for those Jews, but also for many who had remained in Palestine but preferred Greek to Hebrew, the Old Testament had been translated into Greek. That translation was called the Septuagint.

In Isaiah's original prophecy, as recorded in the Hebrew version, the word Isaiah uses is "almah" which means a: young woman. Only in terms of cultural expectation would she have been a virgin, likely so, but not necessarily so. Almah most correctly is to be translated "a young woman." It is not clear how or why it happened, but in the translation from Hebrew to Greek in the Septuagint version of Isaiah, the word almah was changed to "parthenos," which in Greek does mean virgin. The Hebrew Bible never said virgin but the Septuagint did, and Matthew picks it up from there. It is interesting to speculate that, if Matthew had used the Hebraic Bible not the Septuagint, the doctrine of the virgin conception might never have come up as a concept. I think we can say it would **not** have come up, because Matthews's concern is really not with the virginal status of Mary but with what he thought was the need to fulfill a misunderstood translation of Isaiah's prophecy. However Matthew did use the incorrect Septuagint version of Isaiah and the whole "virgin" story evolved.

And yet Matthew's story is so beautifully done, and so humanely recounted when he tells us that Joseph was upset with Mary's pregnancy and considered divorce. A divorce would have been required because in

Jewish law, betrothal, the giving and accepting of the proposal of marriage, was considered to **be** marriage. In the eyes of society they were married. The wedding ceremony which followed betrothal was to publicly celebrate and make clear to the family and friends that this couple is married. Intercourse during betrothal was technically wrong, but it was actually quite common and generally understood that it likely would take place. Why not ...they were married! But Matthew says this did not happen. (1:18)

So, we have three choices by which to explain Mary's pregnancy. First, it was a miraculous conception. Second, Mary was seduced by a Roman soldier and became pregnant by him. Or thirdly, she and Joseph did have intercourse, and she became pregnant by Joseph. The Roman seduction being more likely a slanderous accusation than truth, we put that aside rather quickly. If we also want to put aside a miraculous conception, then the fact that Joseph was a righteous man, and Mary a virgin when they were engaged, would lead us to choose Joseph as Jesus' father.

However we do not need to make this choice simply because it seems to be the most reasonable of the three possibilities. The Gospels include statements in which Joseph is regarded as being Jesus' father; "Is not this Jesus, the son of Joseph, whose father and mother we know?" (John 6:42) "And Mary said to Jesus, 'your father and I have been looking for you.'"(Luke 2:48) "And (Jesus') father and mother were amazed." (Luke 2:33)

The thing is, parentage and virginal birth are not what is of consequential interest to Matthew or Luke who both mention it once and then literally move on to other things. Actually Matthew is mostly concerned in all the details of his story, to show that Jesus' birth is the consequence, the fulfillment, of God's long preparation for the Messiah through all the generations. This intention shines through in the first sentence following the genealogy when Matthew says: "....the birth of the Messiah took place in this way." (1:18) He doesn't say the birth of Jesus, he says the birth of the Messiah, the birth which comes in conclusion to the promise of the Messiah contained in that genealogy. So when Matthew says of Mary, right after the genealogy, "She was found to be with child from the Holy Spirit," (1:18) he is saying the same Holy Spirit who was active in that long history of preparing for the momentous day of Jesus' birth was equally involved in Jesus' birth. This birth is part of a seamless working out of the plan of God. This real intention of Matthew comes forth clearly when he says, "All this took place to fulfill what the Lord had said through the prophet: 'Look, the virgin shall conceive and bear a son, and they shall name him Emmanuel,' which means, "God is with us.'" (1:23) Note those dramatic and intentional four words! Do not miss them because Matthew is making an incredible statement that his whole genealogy and his entire story of Jesus' birth are to tell us that in Jesus, "God is with us!"

We continue Matthew's story in the next chapter.

Chapter Twenty-Seven

Birth in Matthew... continued

Matthew continues his story of Jesus' birth by telling us Joseph was a "righteous man," a technical term indicating he was a man blameless before the law.(1:19) It was also a way of saying that legally Joseph could have secured a divorce with no onus on him but great penalty upon Mary. He is unwilling to do this, perhaps for that reason. Then, it happens in a dream that the angel Gabriel appears to him in the same way he had appeared to Mary. This angelic appearance is a metaphor for the way in which Joseph resolved his inner turmoil. Did the Holy Spirit really help him? I don't know, but I believe it has helped me in many an inner turmoil decision. Ultimately, for whatever reason, aided by the Spirit or not, Joseph chooses to believe her and fulfills the betrothal by marrying her. (1:24) As for Joseph's dream being the source for his decision, his name is Joseph! How else would it happen! Matthew, who ties everything to the Old Testament, is doing that again. In Jewish history, who is the dreamer of dreams? Joseph, whose brothers sold him into slavery and wound up in Egypt. In the Old Testament Joseph interprets dreams. Well, Mary's Joseph does too. He comes to the decision of what to do on the basis of his dream. He will believe Mary and accept her word. That problem being solved, the story can move on.

Matthew records that Jesus was born in Bethlehem. There is no need for a journey from Nazareth to Bethlehem because Joseph and

Mary are residents of Bethlehem. Jesus is born not in a stable, but in a house. (2:11)

Matthew continues his story with the exciting addition of wise men from the East coming to Jerusalem seeking the king of the Jews. They came to King Herod who immediately went on full alert! Roman records show he was crafty, cruel, murderous, and most of all, paranoid. "What? There is another king?" He had to do something about that! Matthew says it was a star that led the wise men. (2:2). Was it a supernova? Was it a comet? Maybe it was a planetary conjunction? Mars, Saturn and Jupiter come close together every 805 years; this did happen in 7-6 BCE, and many have latched on to this. Astrology, which was a kind of preface to our astronomy, was well practiced in the ancient world and in the "East," where the wise men are said to originate, it was particularly used to predict the birth or death of great people. If there was a bright star of whatever kind, it could have excited some eastern astrologers. But the birth of Caesar Augustus was also said to have been heralded by a star; and some commentators say that Matthew appropriates the Augustus star and gives it to Jesus as a way of saying it is not Augustus who is the Lord, but Jesus. That would be very much like Matthew so perhaps they are right. But on the other hand, lots of time has been wasted looking for some literal or historical explanation for the star, while it is really a literary device of Matthew never intended to be taken as an actual fact. Matthew's star is again a metaphor. (Get used to that!) If we want to bring the star of Augustus into it, then Matthew is saying that the birth of Jesus was heralding the birth of someone even more important than Augustus because that star stopped over the place where Jesus lay. (2:10). Now that is undeniably a poetic statement. They knew stars did not stop in the sky! But the star stopping over the place gives a vivid picture, doesn't it? Could the importance of this birth be better said in any other way? Matthew has given us a beautiful metaphor by which to understand the import of what is happening here ....God is entering into the world!

The point Matthew is making is that God was in Jesus from the first day of his life. He does that by telling a story, but it is a story that tells the real story, the one that is present in, with, and under whatever it was that actually did happen. Maybe outwardly it wasn't exactly as Matthew presents it, but however it really did take place, God was part of it in every respect. Jesus is God's Son.

So then did Matthew just create this story? We do not know what sources he may have had in addition to his own creativity, so we cannot say, but we can say that Matthew records for us some things which we know did happen. He says that when Herod heard the news of Jesus' birth he was troubled, "…and all Jerusalem with him." (2:3) Herod was a hated King, and yet the whole city was troubled? Perhaps a bit of political spin here, but Matthew most likely developed this from the fact that just before his death Herod had collected and imprisoned dozens of prominent citizens and left orders that upon his death they would be executed. That was the only way there would be mourning in the land. Well, Matthew tells us Herod's wrath begins boiling, and Joseph has another dream. Matthew loves dreams. In 2:12 the wise men are warned in a dream, and in 2:13 another angelic visitation to Joseph warns him as well. He is to flee to Egypt. Only in Matthew is a flight to Egypt mentioned regarding Jesus. The reason comes clear in 2:15: "This was to fulfill the prophecy." Matthew's account of the slaughter of all children under the age of two in the region of Bethlehem (2:16) is not recorded either in Roman or Jewish records. On the other hand, many murders and massacres were committed by Herod who executed his beloved wife and two of his sons for the very reason Matthew ascribes to him, fear that someone would take his throne. If he killed his wife and sons because he thought they were plotting against him, he would certainly not hesitate to slaughter all the infants in one of his provinces if he feared one of them would succeed him. Matthew's story certainly gets Herod's character right!

Herod dies and the holy family returns from Egypt. (2:19) It is generally thought the flight into Egypt was inserted by Matthew into the birth narrative because he had a problem to solve. He had said Joseph was a resident of Bethlehem, now somehow he has to get them to Nazareth to fulfill the prophecy that Jesus was a Nazarene. What he comes up with is a pretty good way to do it: go to Egypt, then skip Bethlehem on the way back, and head to Nazareth. "...he made his home in a town called Nazareth so that what had been spoken through the prophets might be fulfilled; he shall be called a Nazarene." (2:23)

It is curious that no prophecy anyone has been able to find says the Messiah shall come from Nazareth or that he shall be called a Nazarene. Matthew knows his Scripture well enough, even though he makes a mistake here and there with his fulfilled prophecies. The dreams, the command not to be afraid, those receiving the angelic news believing and doing what they are told--all of that is proper Old Testament protocol and it is represented in good form.

A little aside, how many wise men were there? Matthew's Gospel tells us of the wise men, but the number is not mentioned. The number three comes from an Armenian "Gospel of Jesus' Infancy," which also names them as Melchior, king of Persia; Caspar, King of India; and Balthazar, King of Arabia. That gospel comes from the 4th or 5th century, quite a while after Jesus' birth. It is not part of the New Testament but has become part of the Christmas lore of the church.

Matthew is surely a genius and a great story teller. The whole of Matthew's Infancy narratives may not be the stuff of which history is made. We can never know whether any of this, or what part of it, did or did not happen, but it doesn't matter. Matthew paints a picture of the true reality that God is in Jesus. The visitation of God, come among us in the human Jesus, born of a young women, is all done in fulfillment of a long promised action that God would take when the time was right. Matthew has woven it altogether to make it clear that God is within and behind the event of Jesus' coming among us, whatever the birth details may actually have been.

Those who work so hard trying to sort out fact from fiction in Matthew's story to make it more realistic or amenable to modern day understanding are engaged in a futile occupation. Whatever problems we may have with the birth stories of our Lord, if we have any, they are really our problems, not Matthew's. We want Christmas to be a happy time so we lift up the singing angels, the gift-bearing kings, the star, and all those neat things. While I think we know deep down that they are metaphors, still we celebrate them literally, joyfully, thankfully. And I think we do that because we do understand what Matthew is saying; we do get the images, the pictures he writes in words. He is right. Jesus did fulfill prophecies. As the son of David, he fulfills the long covenant history of Israel, the entire Old Testament from Abraham through David to Jesus, who finally is Immanuel the Messiah, the promised one who in a full and final sense will save his people from their sins.

I love Matthew's metaphorical images. And yet I must admit to being a child of the 21st century, in which I am surrounded by the worldview of our day in which science and physics tell us that dreams may not be merely dreams, but real precursors of something to come. And so, while Matthew is writing metaphors and using mythological images; yet, it is very possible there are real events behind Matthew's stories. I don't know, and it really doesn't matter. To whatever extent they are historically true, metaphysically true, psychologically true does not really matter. I know they are true. We accept it; believe it, because the Holy Spirit has brought us to faith. We too have met the risen Jesus; and like the Gospel authors, we know however he was born, Jesus is the Son of God whose death and resurrection joins all of us into a family in which we are, as Jesus told Nicodemus, "born again."

Now that IS a metaphor! And it is one for which we can sing hallelujah with great joy, for it tells us we are joined to God and each other in a mystical body that reaches back to the beginning of creation and forward to the end of time and the new creation that is to come. That is what Matthew is saying. Let the story live, let the Gospel fill your life with its images, it is all true in the sense that really matters. Thank you Matthew for telling us powerfully that God IS with us!

In the next chapter we turn to Luke's infancy narratives which are much longer and even more detailed than Matthew's.

Chapter Twenty-Eight

Birth of Jesus in Luke

Luke develops the idea of John the Baptist as the forerunner of Jesus, as prophesized by Isaiah. Before appearing to Mary, the angel Gabriel appears to Zacharias, announces the birth of John, and tells him his wife Elizabeth will have a son who is destined to usher in the new era of God. Then Luke presents the story of Mary visiting her relative Elizabeth, and the two unborn boys, Jesus and John, while still in the womb, greet each other. However, it is the birth of Jesus that is the story; and Luke, having achieved his purpose of showing John as the forerunner for Jesus, dismisses him with those abrupt words, "The child grew and became strong in spirit, and he was in the wilderness until the day he appeared publicly to Israel." (1:80). That ends Luke's interest in John the Baptist. He is the forerunner, not the main act, and Luke moves to the main act--the story of Jesus' birth.

Gabriel appears to Mary and says to her, "Greetings favored one! The Lord is with you!" (1:28). In the year 405 Jerome translated the New Testament into Latin, called the Vulgate, and his translation changed Gabriel's greeting into the well-known, "Hail Mary full of grace." While certainly never intended to have such consequences, that change helped bring about the veneration that was soon to be given to Mary in the Roman Catholic Church.

Jerome's mistranslation had to have been an error. None of the original manuscripts of Luke allow such a translation. It was a mistake and clearly should be either, "Hail O favored one," or, "Hail you who have been graced." There is no question it is Luke's intention to say that it was simply God's grace that chose Mary, not any grace within her which would have made her God's choice.   God's grace came upon her in the Holy Spirit in the same manner the Spirit comes upon all of us. We can see this when Luke tells us Mary "...was troubled by such a greeting. 'How can this be?'"(1:34) Something that is true for you and me as well; and we too know in the very depth of our being when we are graced by God that we are not worthy of such a visitation.

Now we enter an interesting situation. Mary's doubt appears to be no different than the doubt with which Zachariah responded to the announcement of Gabriel. This could mean it is a beautifully done literary parallel, a device in which two things are shown to be of equal value or importance. There is, however, a huge difference in that the doubt of Zachariah is met with censure and punishment, and the doubt of Mary receives explanation. Why this difference?

When Gabriel tells Zachariah his wife Elizabeth will conceive a son, he responds with great reasonableness, "How can this be, I am an old man and my wife is getting on in years." (1:8) Very diplomatically put! Gabriel censures him for doubting, and his punishment is the inability to speak until the child is born. But later, when Gabriel appears to Mary and repeats a very close version of the words he had said to Zachariah, her response is nearly the same as that of Zachariah. Mary responds, "How can this be," exactly as Zachariah had, and then says "...since I am a virgin," the opposite and yet again exactly similar to Zachariah who said, "... since we are both old." Both were in effect asking for a sign to prove how this birth can be true in the impossible circumstances of their condition.

Perhaps the conclusion of many scholars is the best answer. There is some evidence that verses 34 and 35 were not in Luke's original version, but that later someone else added those verses. Here is the exchange between Gabriel and Mary: (1:30-38)

> "The angel said to her, "Do not be afraid, Mary, for you
> have found favor with God. 31 And now, you will conceive

in your womb and bear a son, and you will name him Jesus. [32].........." [34] Mary said to the angel, "How can this be, since I am a virgin?" [35] The angel said to her, "The Holy Spirit will come upon you, and the power of the Most High will overshadow you; therefore the child to be born[j] will be holy; he will be called Son of God. [36] And now, your relative Elizabeth in her old age has also conceived a son; and this is the sixth month for her who was said to be barren. [37] For nothing will be impossible with God." [38] Then Mary said, "Here am I, the servant of the Lord; let it be with me according to your word." Then the angel departed from her."

It is striking that if we leave out verses 34 and 35, the story reads much more fluidly: *"The angel said to her, 'Do not be afraid, Mary, for you have found favor with God. [31] And now, you will conceive in your womb and bear a son, and you will name him Jesus....' [32] "Then Mary said, 'Here am I, the servant of the Lord; let it be with me according to your word."*

If we leave verses 34 and 35 in place, the problem of why Gabriel was not consistent in censuring Mary as he had Zachariah remains a puzzling question. Without those verses Mary does not ask for a sign, therefore there is no censure. It could have happened that Luke, or someone else, suddenly realized the story implied that Joseph is Jesus' father....Gabriel merely telling her she is pregnant. So verses 34 and 35 were added to remove that possibility; Mary protests that she is a virgin, and hence Jesus is not the son of Joseph.

If those two verses were added for that reason or some other one, it is very clumsily done but it does show us both the human compilation of the Gospel and the involvement of the whole community in its production,

While the manuscript evidence only suggests that verses 34 and 35 were a later addition; without those two verses Mary gives Gabriel the response that Luke, throughout his Gospel insists all should make when given a spiritual experience. That is, Luke insists we should not question, but simply respond, "Thanks be to God!" Throughout the New Testament praise and joy are appropriate response to God's blessings, and removing those two verses achieves that proper response for Mary. Also, Luke hints throughout his Gospel the possibility that Joseph **was** the biological father of Jesus. Luke neither affirms nor denies this because, either way, he would say the Holy Spirit is still the agency of Jesus' birth and God's presence within Jesus. Luke has no angel visit to Joseph and no second thoughts about the marriage and seems to imply that Mary and Joseph were married soon after Gabriel's visitation; and that in the natural course of events Joseph was the father of Jesus.

As we continue with Luke's birth narrative, it is interesting that the baby Jesus is absent in person. Luke talks about him but we don't really meet Jesus. Luke tells the story in a way that shows us less who Jesus was and more how his birth was a sacred event. In this Luke does a great job, his story moving so seamlessly, we are tempted to forget this is a re-creation of events looking back from a point after the resurrection. We are almost willing to enthusiastically embrace his narrative as the real deal. But if we do, if we take the stories as being literal rather than mythological, there are impossible difficulties.

It is doubtful that the decree of Caesar that the entire world should be registered, or Luke's claim that Quirinius was Governor of Syria during the reign of Herod, are historically correct. But they are beautifully theologically correct, for when Luke says the birth happened when "…the whole world was to be registered" it is again a statement that the birth of Jesus is for all people, the whole world, not just the Jews. And is it not delicious irony that Luke says Jesus was born in Bethlehem because of a decree of the Roman government! God was working out his purposes, not only among Israel and the Jews, but in the whole world. And unwittingly, dear Theophilus, even the Emperor is beholden to God's plan. The involvement of Rome in Jesus' birth continues as Luke tells us the family was living in Nazareth and went from Nazareth to Bethlehem <u>by decree of the Emperor</u>.

When they arrived in Bethlehem there was no room in the inn. If Luke's source was right and Joseph had family in Bethlehem, it is not likely that Joseph would have sought out an inn, for the family would have been offended if Mary and Joseph did not stay with them. If Luke intended this story to be read as fact, would he not have given Joseph a bit more credit as a husband? Surely he would have seen to it they had plenty of time before Mary's delivery to find a place to stay. But Luke does not intend a factual story, and the stable much better fits his dramatic purpose than an inn or a relative's home! The stable is so rich in symbolism, Luke simply could not have left it out. And later Luke tells us Jesus said of himself, "…foxes have dens and birds' nests but the son of Man has no place to rest his head." (9:58) Luke certainly had this in mind when he says the Son of God had no cradle, but a manger.

And then Luke brings in the shepherds (2:8-16). Only Luke mentions shepherds, but they had to be included for the same reason the stable had to be the birthplace. Shepherds were regarded in general as the lowest of the low on the social scale. So Luke is saying the child, this King, is born for everyone, even those of lowest circumstance. Jesus is for you, Luke says, no matter how low your station in life and it cannot get lower than a shepherd! Then Luke brings in the angels. Luke loves angels. And how could there not be an angel choir to herald such a great event! Since this is a momentous birth, in which God is at work in a miraculous and amazing way, of course there are angels. And they sing, "Glory to God in the highest heaven and on earth peace among those whom he favors." (2:14) ("Peace, good will toward men" are in some of the later Latin and Greek texts.)

But Mary is silent. Luke says she kept these things in her heart and pondered on them (2:19) So, thanks to the shepherds, who Luke says told everyone they saw, Jesus' birth did get a little notice in the Bethlehem press. But Mary had nothing to say about it. Perhaps Luke added that in as an explanation for why throughout all four Gospels Mary has little or nothing to say about Jesus, except a single occasion in Mark 3:31, where Mary thinks Jesus has gone out of his mind claiming he is the Messiah.

The circumcision of Jesus is very briefly mentioned. Jesus' presentation required by Jewish law brings the family from Bethlehem to the temple in Jerusalem. There a "righteous man," Simeon, takes the babe in his arms, praises God, and says that Jesus will be "A light of revelation to the Gentiles and glory for his people Israel." (2:-32) Once again we see Luke's concern for the Gentiles. But Simeon's words cast a dark shadow over what was a joyous event when he says, "This child is destined for the falling and rising of many," and, then, to Mary,"...a sword will pierce your own soul too." (2:34) With the perspective provided by looking back from the crucifixion, Luke can correct the Jewish expectation that the Messiah will lead his people on an easy path to glory. Quite the contrary Luke says he will be the center of storm and controversy, which will reveal the secret thought of many hearts and result in the end in a piercing grief for his mother. This is dark stuff, and somewhat strange, for this is the opposite of the majesty, pomp, and glory which announced the coming of the Messiah in Luke's birth narrative.

But is it not very interesting when Luke says, "And the child's **father** and mother were amazed at what was being said about him." (2:33) Father, of course, stands out. Mary and Joseph were both "amazed" at the things Simeon said? After all that had happened? No, this is best considered to be another indication that Luke edited his first draft, which did not include any reference to a virgin birth, but in doing so missed a few of his original comments about Joseph as Jesus' father. We see another indication of that when Luke tells us the only story in the New Testament about Jesus' boyhood. Mary says, "Son, why have you treated us like this? Your **father** and I have been anxiously searching for you." (2:47-50) Does this perhaps show us again that the New Testament was written by the community, bringing together the many experiences and understandings of the community.

In conclusion, while the birth stories were not intended as historical accounts, they were nonetheless intended to be understood as true accounts, as symbols, or containers, which held within them the real meaning of Jesus' birth, the transcendent reality that in Jesus God has come among us. We are dealing in Jesus' birth with something we can only strive to understand; and understanding of the deepest things in life always comes best through pictures, images and stories. That God has come among us in Jesus is too awesome for words. The best that can be done has been done by Matthew and Luke, and we are thankful for what they have given us. We need their images, we need their myths, we need their infancy narratives; for only in them, as the Spirit guides us, are we able to understand the profound truth of what happened in Jesus' birth. God embraces human life and destiny, and in that embrace we are redeemed, and in our redemption we are burnished, illuminated, lifted, saved, forgiven. And given, Paul says, an "eternal weight of glory." (2 Corinthians 4:17)

Let us celebrate Jesus' birth in the way Matthew and Luke tell it, for it is the best way it can be told. Let it be the Christmas miracle it truly is, and let us leave in place all the images which make it possible to tell the miraculous story: the virgin birth, the visitation of angels, a baby Jesus, a manger, shepherds and all the rest. Let us read it, tell it, celebrate it; and as we celebrate, let us say as the Gospels exhort us, Thanks be to God!

Part Five

The Passion Narratives

Chapter Twenty-Nine

Passion of Jesus

As we move into the passion story, Mark will be our guide, with the other Gospels joining in as we continue. But we need first of all to establish a date for the death of Jesus. The best we can do with that is a birth date around the year 4, and the crucifixion, and resurrection, about the years 30-32. It was Jesus' resurrection which brought the Christian church into existence. Immediately after the crucifixion the followers of Jesus were in total disarray, demoralized and fearful. But then, and it happened so quickly it was like an incendiary fire, hundreds and hundreds of those early followers who had been so torn and stricken with grief, suddenly became enthusiastic witnesses to the fact that Jesus had been raised from death and appeared to them.

Such an amazing about-face is astounding, and the only sensible explanation is that they did indeed meet the risen Jesus. Skeptics would say, "Or they imagined they had met him." Forget the skeptics. An imagined resurrection could not possibly have created the fervor and passion that consumed them as they proclaimed the event. But in what way did Jesus appear to them? As we look at passion accounts in the four gospels, we discover they simply do not sing the same song. And unfortunately, no matter how much we try to make the music fit the words, when we listen critically it sounds off key. The four gospels have four different tunes going on that are quite unlike each other. It may be a bit jarring at first as we get into this, but trust me it all comes out in the end to be a beautiful hymn!

Thankfully the period of oral transmission before the gospels were written was not simply a hodgepodge collection of stories about Jesus. A close examination of Mark, the first gospel to put those stories in written form, shows us that they had been collected into groupings rather than isolated segments. A continuous story about the events of Jesus' death had been collected very soon after his resurrection and was used for worship, certainly during Holy week, and perhaps in abbreviated form for the Lords Supper. It was also a type of catechism with which to teach the faith to new converts. When Mark is carefully taken apart, we can see how the oral tradition is the bones or skeleton upon which Mark added the flesh of Peter's recollections and perhaps his own, rearranging to fit his theme. What could have been a Frankenstein of many parts simply joined together, in the gifted hands of Mark, results in a fascinating, beautifully crafted account, from the first sentence, "The beginning of the Gospel of Jesus Christ, the son of God," (1:1)   to the end, when the centurion at the foot of the cross says, "Truly this man was Gods Son!"(15.39)

Mark consistently maintains two major themes: That Jesus is the son of God, and that this fact is never clearly obvious in his ministry. Again and again the crowds witness Jesus' miracles and hear his words, and always some believe and some do not. The second theme, perhaps the most dramatic element in Mark's passion account, is Jesus constant battle with Satan and the powers of evil. In encounter after encounter Jesus is attacked by Satan, and confronted by demons. The battle continues until finally, in his death, when it looks as if he has been defeated, he prevails, not only over Satan and the power of evil, but over death itself. Mark spends little time wondering why Jesus had to die, or in what way his death achieves the purposes of God, simply saying the passion of Jesus, for all its apparent weakness, ends in victory and new life for him and for all those who are in him!

Matthew, Mark, and Luke, do not say it in so many words, but they are clear in showing that the ministry of Jesus all took place in one jam-packed year, the majority of it in Galilee and surrounding environs. For them, when Jesus does leave Galilee for Jerusalem, it is near the end of his ministry, and the beginning of the end of his life. But John, once again the maverick, says Jesus ministry lasted 3 years, and included four visits to Jerusalem. This great difference in the time line of Jesus' life is one of the reasons we are often confused about the events in his ministry.

The synoptic tradition begins the passion of Jesus at the very end of his ministry when he leaves the area of the Galilee for his one and only visit to Jerusalem. He enters Jerusalem on Palm Sunday, immediately enters the Temple and overturns the tables in the temple. Both literally and symbolically, Jesus overturns everything for the religious leaders, who rightly see this action as a direct attack upon them and their power. In the synoptic account, the temple cleansing in the last week of his life is the precipitating cause for his death, as the religious leaders begin to plot on what basis to accuse him, and how to capture him. This leaves it inexplicable why the religious leaders showed such animosity towards Jesus throughout his ministry.

It is quite different in John. Jesus begins his ministry with the temple cleansing, which also begins the opposition of the religious leaders that grows increasingly hostile over the next three years. In John's view this is because Gods presence in Jesus is hidden, and can be recognized only by those to whom the Holy Spirit gives the power to understand. The Jewish religious leaders, not willing to open their minds to the spirit, cannot be brought to faith, and therefore never understand. They focus upon the surface meaning of what Jesus says, and because they miss the spiritual meaning, their hearts become hardened. They follow him around taking notes, hoping to find something in what he says or does that will provide the grounds for his death. This is almost exactly Mark's view as well, although for Mark it all happens within one year.

Another difference between John and the other three is that in the synoptic gospels is not attacking the merchants in the temple; his anger is directed at priests who condone and do not confront the injustice all around them but ignore it, and worry instead about whether their robes are on straight. When Jesus so forcefully upsets the temple the priests get what he is doing and clearly see the finger of Jesus pointing at them. And they don't like it. In the synoptic account that's the proximate cause of Jesus' death.

In huge difference from this, John says Jesus does attack the merchants. Taking a whip, he cries at them "Take these things out of here! Stop making my Father's house a marketplace!" (2:16)   Then when the priests ask him why he was doing this, his enigmatic answer is "Destroy this temple, and in three days I will raise it up." (2; 19)   John is saying the Temple is no longer needed for Jesus is the new temple, and in him God can be approached in prayer by all people. The old temple is no longer valid.

Chapter Thirty

The Lord's Supper

The Passion narrative continues with the Lord's Supper celebration of Jesus and his followers in the upper room. In telling this story the synoptic accounts compare very well with each other. Mark;

> On the first day of Unleavened Bread, when the Passover lamb is sacrificed, his disciples said to him, "Where do you want us to go and make the preparations for you to eat the Passover?" So he sent two of his disciples, saying to them, "Go into the city, and a man carrying a jar of water will meet you; follow him, and wherever he enters, say to the owner of the house, 'The Teacher asks, Where is my guest room where I may eat the Passover with my disciples?' He will show you a large room upstairs, furnished and ready. Make preparations for us there." So the disciples set out and went to the city, and found everything as he had told them; and they prepared the Passover meal. When it was evening, he came with the twelve. (14: 12-17)

Mark says Jesus sent "two disciples" to secure the room, and then, as if not realizing what he had just said, adds, "When evening came Jesus arrived with the 12." Not 12 less two. Matthew is nearly the same; however he abbreviates it a little by leaving out the man carrying the water jar and the dinner taking place in an upstairs room. Luke leaves in the details of the water jug and upstairs room but instead of "two disciples" as in Mark, Luke names the two as Peter and John. All three agree they found everything as Jesus had told them and prepared the Passover, and all three agree that Jesus told the disciples to tell the man they met that "the Teacher" asks "Where the room is for me and my disciples to eat the Passover?" Some scholars think "the Teacher" may imply the man they met was also a follower of Jesus, and possibly had been given advance warning. To secure a large room ready and prepared for a Passover celebration at the last minute would be very difficult.

Unless, as early tradition says, the supper was held in the home of Mary a wealthy widow who was a strong supporter of Jesus and his ministry. It likely was the same room the disciples used after the crucifixion, when they hid out behind locked doors, for the room was used as a meeting place for the early church, soon after the Resurrection.

The Synoptic Gospels tell us Jesus and his disciples gathered in the upper room to celebrate the Passover, the highest Jewish festival, a remembrance and celebration of deliverance from bondage in Egypt. John disagrees, and John has much on his side of the argument. The Passover always fell on the 14th of Nisan, the day itself changing but usually falling in March–April. The Paschal lamb was to be killed between 3 and 5 o'clock on the 13 of Nisan. Passover began at sunset of the 13th. This is important because 5 minutes before sunset it would be the 13th of Nisan, 5 minutes after it would be the 14th. That is what makes the following mystery so interesting:

The synoptic Gospels agree in saying Jesus kept the Passover with his disciples that night, during which the Lords supper was introduced. Then they left for the Mount of Olives, where Jesus was arrested later that same night. He was condemned to death early the next morning, and crucified and died before sunset the next day. This is very important chronology, for according to the three synoptic gospels, Jesus died on the day of Passover, the 14th of Nissan. John puts everything 24 hours earlier, in which case it could not have been a Passover meal they shared in the upper room. If John is right the crucifixion took place not on the day of the Passover, but on the "Day of Preparation for the Passover." (19:14) According to John, Jesus died on 13th Nisan, between 3 and 5 o'clock, the exact moment when the paschal lambs were being sacrificed, and before the Passover itself, which did not begin until sundown. Who is right? The answer is somewhat momentous, so we need to look at it very closely

If the Last Supper was a Passover meal, then Jesus' trial and crucifixion took place during the week-long holiday, and the Jewish authorities, who were involved in Jesus trial and crucifixion, would have committed a most unlikely action. Holding trials and carrying out executions during Passover would have put them in total violation of Jewish law, and it is hard to imagine that if that is what happened, Jesus' followers would not have made the most of it! On the other hand, they did not have the 24/7 news coverage we suffer in our day, and may not have realized what was happening until it was too late. But even so, the synoptic accounts depict something that is very unlikely if the trial was held on the day of the Passover, but which would fit very well into a trial held on the day before Passover! We need to look further at the problems of the synoptic account of that most unholy night.

As they begin their version of the Passover/ Last supper meal the synoptic version does not mention the presence of women, even though their absence would be highly unusual for a Passover celebration. Of course women may have been present, but simply not mentioned. Jesus included many women within his group of closest followers, and they were highly visible and important in his ministry. They almost certainly would have been there. This is not a big problem, but it is interesting.

What is a big problem for the synoptic claim, that the crucifixion took place on the Passover, is that it is very difficult to believe that on the day of the highest festival of the Jewish faith, the high court would convene a special session to order an execution, Simply getting the court assembled on that most holy night would have been a logistic nightmare. And there are other problems with the synoptic account. For example, strict rules were in place to guide the deliberations of the Sanhedrin: one of them stated that all meetings were to be held in the Gizith, a special chamber within the Temple. They were not to meet anywhere else. Mark however claims the Sanhedrin met, and the trial was held, in the house of the high priest. (14:53, 4) Matthew says Jesus was taken to the house of Caiaphas the High Priest, where the scribes and the elders were gathered together, and that on the next morning, the priests held another meeting. (26:57)

That raises another problem, for in addition to the prescription that all meetings were to be held in the Gizith, in order to temper down emotions, and allow time for more outspoken opinions to cool down, it was required that when all testimony had been heard, the court was to observe a 24 hour waiting time before the verdict could be determined. The synoptic account claims, in violation of this rule, that the Sanhedrin pronounced the death sentence immediately upon convening. Deliberation and verdict, within minutes of each other, not following the prescribed waiting time of twenty four hours! That would certainly have received objection even from some members of the court itself; think Nicodemus and Joseph of Arimathea!

But the most difficult objection to the synoptic view, that this all occurred on the day of the Passover, is that, as Jewish scholars have long insisted, the Sanhedrin was prohibited from holding a trial which might result in a death sentence, on the eve of the Sabbath, or upon the day of a festival observance. If the supper, the arrest, and the trial all took place on the day of the Passover, every prohibition of the Law is violated, whereas no violation occurred if it all took place on the day before the Passover, as John says. Perhaps these, and other difficulties, are understandable in the confusion of that night, but taken together they do tend to undercut the synoptic assertion that the meal in the upper room was a Passover meal. The evidence is not clear and perhaps the synoptic account is to be doubted.

There are fewer reasons to doubt John's account, and many reasons to support it. First, John is very much in accord with what the early community taught about the death of Jesus being a sacrifice in which his death brings our redemption; just as in Jewish theology the Passover lamb brought Israel's redemption. That theme of the lamb, and Jesus being the Lamb of God, is present in John's gospel from the very first scene, when Jesus comes to John the Baptist to be baptized, and John seeing him coming, says, "Behold the lamb of God who takes away the sins of the world." John is consistent from that point up to the end of the gospel when Jesus tells Peter, "Feed my sheep, feed my lambs." (21; 17 ff)

It is also of interest that in the synoptic account the only foods mentioned are bread and wine, the basic requirements of any Jewish meal. But if the supper was a Passover meal, why is there no mention of the Passover lamb, or the bitter herbs, or the four cups of wine, all required components of that meal? Of course it could be they were simply not mentioned, but it does score another point for John's view! Would that we could settle this argument conclusively, but we cannot; there are credible adherents for both views and it is simply not absolutely certain whether it was or was not a Passover meal. What we do know is that, whichever it was, the meal included within it what we call the Lord's Supper, and to that we turn in the next chapter.

Chapter Thirty-One

The Lord's Supper in the Gospels

The events are somewhat muddled and uncertain regarding whether the meal was a Passover meal or not, but what has come to be called the Lord's Supper was part of the meal Jesus celebrated with his followers. The earliest account of that meal is not that of the gospels but of Paul, whose account brings additional considerations for understanding that night. Paul says:

> *"For I received from the Lord what I also handed on to you, that the Lord Jesus on the night when he was betrayed took a loaf of bread, and when he had given thanks, he broke it and said, 'This is my body that is for you. Do this in remembrance of me.' In the same way he took the cup also, after supper, saying, 'This cup is the new covenant in my blood. Do this, as often as you drink it, in remembrance of me.' For as often as you eat this bread you proclaim the Lords death until he comes."* (1Cor 11:23-26)

Paul was convinced that what he recounts are the actual words of Jesus at the supper; "I got this from the Lord," he says, claiming it as a firsthand account from Jesus himself. In the early community the supper was celebrated to remember that in Jesus, we have been brought into the family of God, and made part of the ancient covenant God had made with his people. Paul says that we are to remember, celebrate, and give thanks as we share the supper. And to realize it is not taking the bread and wine which forgives our sins, but that our sins have been forgiven in Jesus death and resurrection, and in the supper, we remember and give thanks for what Christ has done. In the communal act of sharing the bread and wine with one another, remembering what has been done for us all in Jesus; we strengthen our own faith and that of one another

When we celebrate the sacrament, we are doing just what Jesus asked us to do--remember what he has done--remember what it cost him to do it--realize that it was done for us. Paul uses the word "anamnesis, "which means "as a remembrance." He does not use "mnemosunon," which means as a memorial sacrifice; so when the Lords supper is celebrated, it is not a sacrifice being repeated. Neither, however, is it merely a memorial. It is a celebration of what has been achieved for us in the death of Jesus. Interesting only Paul tells us Jesus says "do this." Paul's letters were written before the gospels, which all incorporate Paul's account of the Lords Supper into their own, each changing it a little and adding their own interpretation of what it means. (John's Gospel does not include the Lord's Supper)

Before Paul the words of Jesus had become set, taking on the liturgical form we still use today. At first the Communion was celebrated as part of a larger meal; the early community understanding the original supper as having been part of a meal. This was to change, and the supper becomes attached to the Lords Day worship. The needs of the institutional church and practicality at work!

We look now at the differences in the accounts, using Paul as our base: (see above for Paul's words)

Mark (14:22-25) is the closest to Paul.
Mark recounts it this way: *While they were eating, he took a loaf of bread, and after blessing it he broke it, gave it to them, and said, "Take; this is my*

body." Then he took a cup, and after giving thanks he gave it to them, and all of them drank from it. He said to them, "This is my blood of the covenant, which is poured out for many. Truly I tell you, I will never again drink of the fruit of the vine until that day when I drink it new in the kingdom of God."

Notice that while Paul says *"This is my body that is for you. "* Mark omits the words *"that is for you"*. And while Paul says *"This cup is the new covenant..."* Mark omits "new" from the phrase. Mark also adds a sentence *"truly I tell you, I will never again drink of the fruit of the vine until that day when I drink it new in the kingdom of God."*

Matthew (26:26-29)

Matthew's version goes like this: *"While they were eating, Jesus took a loaf of bread, and after blessing it he broke it, gave it to the disciples, and said, "Take, eat; this is my body." Then he took a cup, and after giving thanks he gave it to them, saying, "Drink from it, all of you; for this is my blood of the covenant, which is poured out for many for the forgiveness of sins. I tell you, I will never again drink of this fruit of the vine until that day when I drink it new with you in my Father's kingdom."*

Matthew is in considerable agreement with Mark's account, also omitting the word "new" from the covenant. But Matthew adds: *which is poured out for many for the forgiveness of sins.* This is a big change, for while he does not exactly say it, he introduces the possibility of interpreting the supper itself as granting forgiveness of sins. This was in no way the original idea of the Lords Supper, but Matthew had a reason for how he puts it. As people of the Jewish covenant began joining the church; they were imbued with sacrificial concepts, the Paschal lamb, the temple sacrifices, etc., and they best understood Jesus death in those terms. Matthew helps this along by saying "yes Jesus blood too is a sacrifice, shed for many for the remission of sins." Thereby Matthew connects the blood of the "old covenant" with the blood of Jesus in the new covenant.

Luke (22:14-20)

Luke says: *When the hour came, he took his place at the table, and the apostles with him. He said to them, "I have eagerly desired to eat this Passover with you before I suffer; for I tell you, I will not eat it until it is fulfilled in the kingdom of God." Then he took a cup, and after giving thanks he said, "Take this and divide it among yourselves; for I tell you that from now on I will not drink of the fruit of the vine until the kingdom of God comes." Then he took a loaf of bread, and when he had given thanks, he broke it and gave it to them, saying, "This is my body, which is given for you. Do this in remembrance of me." And he did the same with the cup after supper, saying, "This cup that is poured out for you is the new covenant in my blood.*

Luke writes after Matthew; but close in time to the break which was occurring between Jewish and Gentile Christians. He sticks close to Mark and Paul, but reverses the order of bread and wine, and makes it clear Jesus did not partake of either. As do Mark and Paul, Luke understands the Lords Supper as a meal pointing toward that day when it will be for Jesus, and for all of us who follow him, a victory meal, as the Kingdom of God for which he died becomes a triumphant reality.

The primary reason there are differences in the accounts of the three gospels is due to their being written at different times in the life of the community, and for different audiences. Despite the need this placed upon the authors, they remain very similar in their agreement; that the essential meaning and purpose of the supper is to remember that Jesus death is made on our behalf brings us forgiveness of our Sin, and the restoration of our relationship with God in the new covenant in him.

Chapter Thirty-Two

The Passion continues

When the supper was over, or if John is correct, after Jesus washes the feet of the disciples and delivers an extensive message known as the "upper room discourse," they sang a hymn and left for the garden of Gethsemane. (John 14-16) When the gospels tell us what Jesus said in his prayer in the garden, it is difficult to know what their source was for this, since it is said no one was with him. They were all asleep. But what Jesus prayed is really not the point. The falling asleep, running away, deserting him, is intended to show us how Jesus must, and does, achieve the will and purpose of God on his own. No human help is possible. Mark tells us Jesus makes three trips from private prayer, back to his disciples because he is struggling so hard, with accepting God's will for him. Mark shows us a very human Jesus, in a great deal of pain and anguish, wishing he could avoid what is coming.

Matthew agrees with Mark that Jesus makes three trips back to the sleeping disciples. Then he develops this into a neat contrast between Jesus, the Son of God in whom the spirit is victorious, and the merely human disciples in whom their flesh is victim to their humanness, lack of sleep, and having consumed to much wine. (26:36-46)

Luke does his best to ignore and remove all of that. He doesn't want a human Jesus he wants a Son of God; so he changes three trips into one trip, and brings in a miraculous element: as angels come and give him strength. Luke tries to bring the miraculous into everything he says about Jesus. It's his way of indicating that Jesus is the son of God. (22:39-46)

John's gospel does not include Jesus prayer in the garden. John simply says that after the supper they went to "a place where there was a garden" and there he is arrested. (18:2-12) In John's account of the arrest, Jesus remains in control of what happens, and the soldiers hesitate to arrest Jesus even when, twice, he says he is the one they are seeking. (18:6, 8).

All four Gospels say that one of Jesus' disciples cut off the ear of the high priest's slave, but only in John are these two individuals explicitly named, Simon Peter, and Malchus. (18:10) Only in Luke does Jesus restore the man's ear. (22:50) Good old Luke loves his miracles! In Luke, Jesus interrupts the action, by asking, "Judas, would you betray the Son of Man with a kiss?" and the arrest of Jesus follows immediately. (22:48) Mark is the only one to include the most interesting detail; *"A young man was following Him, (Jesus) wearing nothing but a linen sheet over his naked body, they seized him but he pulled free of the linen sheet and escaped naked."* (14:51)Another detail, provided only by John, makes the interesting comment that Judas led a "detachment"' of Roman soldiers, together with the temple police, to arrest Jesus. (18:2) this means the religious authorities had already involved the civil authorities, and therefore, had to have made a charge against Jesus, even before the trial which follows his arrest. That is VERY interesting!

It is impossible to know exactly what happened in Jesus arrest. Each gospel presents different remembered details, and much is rearranged in composition. But whatever the precise details might have been, there is total agreement in all four that in all the events which unfold, Jesus takes the path ordained for him by God. And he walks it alone, without friends. Jesus is abandoned, forsaken, damned ...in our place. Don't miss that. All four Gospels make it clear; without what Jesus does in our place, we would be the one forsaken, alone, damned.

The Trial
After the arrest they take Jesus to the High Priest, Chief Priests, and Sanhedrin, (council of elders) who find Jesus guilty of blaspheming God.

The punishment prescribed in the Hebrew Bible for blasphemy is to be stoned to death (Lev 24:10-23). But that's only true if the Jews do it. Jesus was put to death by the Romans. The charge brought against him was not blasphemy, about which Rome really could care less, but sedition. He was accused by the religious leaders of claiming to be king in opposition to Caesar. Rome did care about that, and the punishment for sedition was crucifixion.

At the trial, slight differences are seen in the gospel accounts. In Mark, Jesus directly admits that he is "the Christ, the Son of the Blessed." (14:61-62) In Matthew he is more cryptic; "you have said so, but I tell you from now on you will see the son of Man seated at the right hand of Power and coming on the clouds of heaven" (26:64) Luke says Jesus replies; "If I tell you, you will not believe and if I question you, you will not answer. But from now on the Man will be seated at the right hand of the Power of God." (22:67) So except for Mark, in which Jesus does admit he is the son of God, there is very little difference in the synoptic accounts. But remember the first line of the Mark's Gospel; "The good news of Jesus Christ the Son of God." So it fits right in for Mark to have Jesus say he is the Son of God.

In John, immediately after the arrest in the garden, Jesus is taken to Annas, Caiaphas' father-in law. (18:12) Then John inserts the first part of Peter's denial, then leaves Peter and returns to Jesus trial before Annas, then back again to Peter for his second and third denial after which Jesus is taken before Pilate. (33-38) As Jesus stands before Pilate, he responds to Pilate's question, "Are you king of the Jews?" by saying "You say that. You say I am a king. To this end I was born, and for this cause I came into the world, that I should bear witness unto the truth. Every one that is of the truth hears my voice." (18:37ff) Then Pilate makes the famous comment: "What is truth?" (18:38)

At this point, Luke, alone among the gospels, puts a little interlude into Pilate's questioning by telling us Pilate sends Jesus to Herod Antipas, the tetrarch of Galilee, who was in Jerusalem for the Passover. (23:6-12). Luke says Herod wanted to see one of the miracles of Jesus he had heard about; but Jesus would not even speak to him, so Herod put a robe on him and sent him back to Pilate. (23:8ff)

Omitting that interlude of Luke, all four gospels tell the same story of Jesus before Pilate. Pilate states that Jesus is innocent, and tries to free him by using a Passover custom of releasing a prisoner. Pilate gives the crowd the choice between freeing Jesus, or the criminal Barabbas, whom to his surprise is the one they choose. Then Pilate sends Jesus to be crucified.

In lands occupied by the Romans, the death penalty could only be carried out with the approval of the local Roman governor. Mark and Matthew explicitly say Jesus was handed over to Roman soldiers to be crucified. Luke and John, more ambiguously allow the interpretation that Pilate handed Jesus over to the Jewish authorities to carry out the cruci-fixion: *"and he handed Jesus over as they wished. "*(Luke 23:25) *"Then he handed him over to them to be crucified."* (John19:16) No, Luke and John may have wanted to bash the religious leaders a bit, but it was the Romans who crucified Jesus not the Jews.

Before being crucified condemned prisoners were often mocked, beaten and scourged, both as part of their punishment, and to weak-en them enough to hasten their death. Since Jesus was condemned for claiming to be "King of the Jews," the soldiers mock him with the symbols of royal power including a scarlet (or purple) cloak, a crown (of thorns), and a reed (instead of a scepter). (Matthew 27:29), (Mark 15:17), (John 19:2, 5) Luke does not have this scene, merely saying that after the choice of Barabbas, Jesus was led away to be crucified. (23:26)

It is sadly but powerfully stated in all four gospels that Jesus is de-serted by his disciples. They run, abandoning not only their loyalty to Jesus, but to themselves, to their word, their intentions, everything. They desert him. And Jesus is left to the care of strangers. The synoptic ac-counts agree that a stranger, Simon of Cyrene, is made to carry Jesus' cross. Mark uses a forceful word, saying, they "compelled him to carry the cross." It is a carefully chosen word for Mark, for he uses that same precise word to describe discipleship. Mark says we are compelled if we follow Jesus, to pick up our cross and follow him. It is a tough road we are given in discipleship, a road of service, perhaps suffering, but a road down which each of us must carry our own cross. However in doing so we are carrying it for Jesus. When Mark uses compel for discipleship it is probably an intentional reference to the crucifixion still to come. Matthew and Luke pick this up from Mark, and their account is almost identically the same.

But once again John disagrees with the synoptic account. He says, "So they took Jesus, carrying the cross by himself." (19:17) There is no Simon of Cyrene. Then, almost as if Mark knew that John was disagreeing with him, Mark shows us how certain he is of his facts by adding "A certain man from Cyrene, Simon, the father of Alexander and Rufus." (15:21) Matthew and Luke, who agree with Mark in saying Simon carried Jesus' cross; do not include this authenticating paternal detail. Maybe they hesitated because John is so certain that Jesus carried his own cross and emphasizes it by saying; "The man who saw it has given testimony, and his testimony is true. He knows that he tells the truth, and he testifies so that you also may have faith." (19:35) John seems almost to be saying, you are wrong Mark! Perhaps intimidating both Matthew and Luke, who then back down just a bit!

So who is right? Who carried the cross? It really does not have to be one of the other, both John and the synoptic accounts can be right. The Romans were incredibly cruel when it came to crucifixion. First a severe beating was administered, and then the victim was forced to carry his cross to the crucifixion site. The "cross" that was carried was not the cross as usually depicted, an upright beam, and a cross beam, joined in one piece. The upright beam was already at the site. Those to be crucified carried the cross beam only, called the patibulum. Then, at the site of the crucifixion, the victim would be nailed to the patibulum, which was then pulled into place on the upright beam of the cross. So it could certainly be that prior to his crucifixion, Jesus carried the cross beam for some of the distance, but then, so severely fatigued he could not continue all the way, Simon was forced to assist him. In this case both recollections would be correct.

On the other hand we know that John loves to give a theological explanation of everything Jesus did or said. John could be underscoring the insistence so present in his Gospel, that Jesus was in control of everything, and that he went to his death alone, without any help. I prefer this way of looking at it, but in the end it doesn't really matter. The meaning of Jesus death is not in the minutiae details, but in the united witness of the Gospels, Paul, the entire New Testament, that it is in Jesus death that we find our forgiveness and redemption.

Chapter Thirty-Three

Crucifixion

They take Jesus to Golgotha, the "Place of the Skull." (Mark 15:22) There is little more than confusion and uncertainty regarding where Golgotha actually was. The letter to the Hebrews tells us Jesus was crucified "outside the gate" (13:12) and most scholars consider it to have taken place on an abandoned stone quarry just outside of the walled city of Jerusalem. In the late first century, the city was enlarged and new walls built to the north and west, almost certainly bringing the site of Jesus' crucifixion and burial inside the city of Jerusalem.

There is much less difficulty in locating the site of Jesus' burial. In the fourth century the Church of the Holy Sepulcher was built on the most likely burial site, as identified by the Emperor Constantine's mother Helena. She based her decision in part upon the fact that, until the year 66, the first Christian community gathered to worship at that site. In the year 70, when the Romans destroyed Jerusalem, they erected a temple to Venus one that spot. After his conversion, the Emperor Constantine tore that shrine down, and in 326, he built the "Church of the Resurrection" on that site. This church, destroyed by Muslims in 1009, rebuilt by the Crusaders in 1149, currently remains as the Church of the Holy Sepulcher, with some portions of the original 4th century church still within its walls and floors. The Greek Orthodox, Roman Catholic and Armenian Apostolic Church share responsibility for the care of the site. Over the centuries the prolific use of incense, candles, and holy paraphernalia darkened the walls with soot and wax, and lack of maintenance made the tomb a very unsatisfactory place for most visitors. (A multi-million dollar clean-up in 2017 remedied this situation.)

In 1867, a tomb was discovered just slightly north of the Damascus Gate in a lovely quiet garden. Basing their decision partly upon Mary's question of "the gardener" when she found the tomb to be empty, this tomb, called the "Garden Tomb," was quickly endorsed as the more likely burial place by many prominent theologians. Tourists immediately adopted it as the preferred site for Jesus' burial. Alas no! Beautiful, quiet and secluded though it is, archaeological evidence dates this tomb as having been constructed in the 7th-8th centuries, eliminating the Garden tomb from possibility as the burial place of Jesus.

However, the crucifixion came before the burial, and it took place on Golgotha, wherever it actually was. Before his crucifixion, Jesus, subjected to severe beatings, arrived at the site of the crucifixion exhausted, weak and terribly beaten down. When he is lifted up on the cross hatred is screamed at him. The taunts of the crowd and the religious leaders rail at him with jeers and obscenities, as if they were possessed by demons. Jesus had battled against the power of evil throughout his ministry, so it was in no way a stretch for the early church to identify the cries of the crowd as being the laughter and glee of Satan and his minions, who thought that they had won after all. Well, so it did appear! Jesus is hoisted up, exhausted and weak, a badly beaten man already near death from his wounds.

The suffering of Jesus is incredibly severe; but terrible as it was the suffering of Jesus that resulted from his beating and his agony on the cross does not capture the depth of what is taking place in his death. Through the centuries, especially during the Lenten season, the church has nearly identified the suffering of Jesus as being the whole of what took place on the cross. But that is not the witness of the Gospels, which tell us the real depth of Jesus' suffering was not the physical suffering. It was the spiritual desolation, the emotional sense of loneliness, the suffering that we all know to be the worst kind there is--betrayal by those we love or trust. It was his abandonment not only by his friends, but also by his father: "Why have you forsaken me?"

The Gospels tell us Jesus' suffering came from his deliberate taking on of the sin of the world. He took upon himself that which bears down upon every human being, the sin that always results in what we know so well--hatred, anger, selfishness, self-centeredness, bullying--the twisted evil spirit at the heart of it all. Every bit of that assaults Jesus as he hangs there. All of that is what Jesus bore on the cross. All of that is what he heard screamed at him. The early church got it right; it was Satan and his minions at work in that crowd, their voices screaming the loudest, as they cackled and laughed in vain effort to discredit his death and his sacrifice. They did their best to deny that what was taking place on Golgotha was part of the plan Jesus and God had agreed on from the beginning. But it was. His was not sentimental suffering; it was beyond suffering, so much more than suffering, something so deep, difficult and beyond understanding that before what is happening on the cross, we can only bow our heads in awe and wonder.

Yes, it was a horrible form of death, and Jesus suffered intense agony. It was a terrible scene--Jesus mocked, scorned, despised, the religious leaders crying out, "If you are the son of God, save yourself!" This scene at the crucifixion is the final illustration of the Gospels as to the blindness of the religious leaders. By this time in Jesus' ministry, in Mark's terms, their hearts were hardened, they were caught up in themselves, and they assume Jesus' primary objective would be the same as theirs--to save himself. They cannot understand that the whole reason he hangs there is to save them, not himself. That is beyond their capability to understand; and so for them it seemed that if he could not save himself, he lacks the power to do so.

But it was not only the religious leaders who screamed at him; the power of Evil, for which Jesus was giving his life, was equally on stark and vivid display in the crowd that stood around him. Their screams as they mocked him show us that the truest insight to the crucifixion of Jesus is that no one understood what was happening here. Until, writing years after the resurrection, finally understanding what did happen in this death, Mark, John, Matthew and Luke realize it must be made clear that what is taking place is not what it looked to be, not what at the time even they thought it was. No, God was at work on Golgotha. But that was something they came to know only looking back after the resurrection. And it is with that new understanding they tell the story of what REALLY happened in Jesus' crucifixion.

Matthew, Mark, and Luke record that a Roman "centurion" stood near the cross and witnessed the death of Jesus. (Mark 15: 39, Matt 27:54 Luke 23:47) After saying that, their accounts of the event diverge. Mark begins the clarification of what really took place that day by telling us that the centurion, when he witnesses the death of Jesus, cries out, "Truly this Man was the Son of God!" (15:39) Mark records no extraordinary events taking place to precipitate this statement, except maybe the three hours of darkness. (15:33) It is striking how consistent Mark is to the thrust of his Gospel, from the first line, the first verse, "The beginning of the Gospel of Jesus Christ the Son of God," to the centurion standing beneath the cross, saying again, "Truly this Man was the Son of God!" Mark powerfully ends as he began, with the main assertion of the Christian faith, that Jesus is the Son of God.

Mark is consistent to his whole Gospel in saying that this truth is not revealed to the centurion by any act of Jesus. There was none. There was only weakness. It was in this weakness that the centurion comes to understand who Jesus is. The centurion is alone in this discovery, no one else who is present understands this, which is typical of Mark. Throughout his Gospel he maintains that unless the Spirit reveals it we cannot understand the things of God. The remark of the centurion could only have been made because the Holy Spirit gave him the ability to see that truth. Perhaps Mark is saying that because the disciples have deserted Jesus, and others must step up, the centurion too takes the disciples' place in bearing witness to what is really happening in Jesus' death. As usual for Mark, it is truly masterfully done.

We need not look at Matthew's version of that night. As Matthew copied his crucifixion story from Mark, he follows Mark's lead exactly, except for Jesus' words from the cross which we will look at later. Luke is another matter, for while he also copied from Mark, he had other sources as well and puts those sources into use. Luke, the one who throughout his Gospel loves the transcendent and supernatural, is uncharacteristically restrained as he tells us the centurion simply says, "Certainly this was an innocent man."(23:47) However, Luke's entire approach to Jesus' passion is that Jesus was innocent of all charges; so, for Luke to have the centurion say, "This man was innocent" fits his thrust, that Jesus is an innocent victim.

It had to have been wonderfully helpful to Luke's missionary effort that it was a Roman who echoed Pilate and pronounced Jesus innocent of the false charges of the religious leaders! It was important as well for the Roman Theophilus to know that Jesus was not the revolutionary and seditious criminal he was said to be by his enemies. This shows us another example of how the purpose of the authors shapes the tradition to fit his needs.

John's Gospel is much more realistic about Roman soldiers, especially hardened centurions. John says: *When the soldiers had crucified Jesus, they took his clothes and divided them into four parts, one for each soldier. They also took his tunic; now the tunic was seamless, woven in one piece from the top. So they said to one another, "Let us not tear it, but cast lots for it to see who will get it." This was to fulfill what the scripture says, "They divided my clothes among themselves, and for my clothing they cast lots." And that is what the soldiers did."* (19:23-25)

If we read the Synoptic account of the crucifixion literally it seems strange that the centurion, after directing the brutal beating of Jesus, should suddenly do an about face and proclaim him an innocent man, or, even more unlikely, the Son of God. Does it not seem more likely that, as John says, following the beatings they laughingly joined in the mockery of the crowd, and then, ripping the robe from him, threw dice to win it? There is no way to know who is right here in an historical sense, because each Gospel modifies the story of what happened in a way that fits their theme and best presents their point of view.

Then Jesus' female disciples are finally included in the account. They absolutely must be included because they are truly more important in Jesus' death and burial than the eleven disciples themselves. The group of women who come to the cross includes Mary Magdalene, Mary the mother of James, and Salome. Unlike the disciples who ran in fear, the women go with Jesus to Golgotha, stay with him as he hangs there, and remain until he dies. Friends and disciples of the closest and dearest kind, they stick with him until the body is taken down. Then, departing the crucifixion, they get together later and plan one more act of love; to come to the tomb on the first day of the week to anoint Jesus' body with spices.

We cannot leave the crucifixion story without looking at the words of Jesus from the cross. Those who are of a certain age will remember the three hour Good Friday observances of years ago, which almost always were built around the seven words from the cross. Were there actually seven words? Not in any one gospel. There are seven only when all four gospels are woven together; and without that harmonization they completely disagree about what Jesus said.

Mark records only one word (15:34)

"My God, My God, why have you forsaken me? "

While this is very dark, it is in keeping with the thrust of Mark's gospel that Jesus dies in our place, and therefore God's judgement upon sin and evil results in his death. Taking our place Jesus suffers what would otherwise be our fate, and Jesus dies as we would have to die--alone, abandoned, and accursed. Could anything capture that better than Mark's one word from the cross *"My God, My God, why have you forsaken me"*?

Then, in an incredibly dramatic statement, Mark says the curtain of the temple, which in Jewish worship separated the priests from those who were worshipers, was torn in two, from top to bottom! The curtain is no longer to be a barrier between us and God for in the death of Jesus we now have direct access to God. The curtain is torn from the TOP to the bottom! What a dramatic way to say it is God who does it! Powerful image!

Matthew agrees with Mark, (27:46) and only those two record that Jesus spoke in Aramaic "Eloi, Eloi, lema sababachthani", which is generally regarded as evidence of the early date and accuracy of Mark. As for Matthew, who always shows how Jesus fulfills the Old Testament prophecies regarding the Messiah, Jesus quotes from Psalm 22, regarded at the time as referring to the Messiah. Then, Matthew tells us before Jesus uttered his last word, "....the earth shook...tombs opened... and the bodies of the saints arose." (27:51,52) Matthew alone claims this miraculous event and while it is impossible to accept this as historical, it is again entirely in line with Matthew's overall presentation of Jesus as being in fulfillment of the Old Testament prophecies:. He is quoting from Isaiah, "Your dead shall live, and their corpses shall rise. Oh, dwellers in the dust awake and sing for joy! For your dew is radiant dew, and the earth will give birth to those long dead." (Isaiah 26; 19)

Luke also copied Mark, but says he used other sources as well, and is perhaps indebted to them for his three words on the cross:

> Luke 23:34: *Father, forgive them, for they do not know what they are doing*
> Luke 23:43: *Truly, I tell you, today you will be with me in paradise*
> Luke 23:46: *Father, into your hands I commend my spirit.*

Since Luke copied from Mark, he certainly knew Mark's word, "*My God, My God...*" but he leaves it out and puts in its place "*Father, into Thy hands I commend my spirit.*" Luke could not handle Jesus' agony in the garden, and here too, he doesn't want to face the utter depths of Jesus' humiliation. Perhaps to be abandoned by God seemed too impossible for Luke, who needs to make it clear in this place, as he does throughout his

Gospel, that Jesus is the Son of God. Since abandonment, agony and humiliation does not fit with a powerful Son of God, Luke leaves it out. He just could not bear the thought of it. He does not want to allow Jesus to be that human!

However, Luke does show us once again his main concern; Jesus is innocent! The first word, "Forgive them, they don't know what they do" is not only a statement of Jesus' innocence, but also a statement that Jesus has the relationship with his father to allow him to ask this of God. Then Luke introduces Jesus' conversation with the thieves, another demonstration of his innocence; for while the two thieves are guilty as charged, Jesus is not. Then when he promises the thief, "Today you will be with me in paradise," Luke is again showing us Jesus is the powerful Son of God--so close to God so much a part of God that he could speak for God, knowing God would honor that promise. And in that same sense, Luke's last word from the cross for the last time confirms that relationship with God; *"Father, into your hands I commend my spirit."*

In John's gospel Jesus also uttered three words:

> John 19:26–27: Woman, here is your son." "Here is your mother."
> John 19:28: I thirst.
> John 19:29-30: It is finished.

John, who is the only disciple to claim he was present at the crucifixion, relates an amazingly realistic version of what took place. As Jesus looks down, seeing John there, and then his mother as well, Jesus commits her to John. This is unusual, for normally the task of caring for the mother would be the responsibility of the next eldest son. It is possible that Jesus is concerned with Mary's spiritual care, and at that point his brother James, the next eldest, was not yet a believer. As beautiful and touching a story as this is, we must note that none of the three Synoptic Gospels mention that Jesus' mother was at the cross. Acts 1:14, Luke says that Jesus' mother was one of the groups of followers who regularly met together for prayer. However, except for that comment, there is almost nothing about her in the Synoptic Gospels. But note too, none of the Synoptic authors were at the crucifixion while John was. So his account would seem to have precedence.

Regarding who did stand beneath the cross, in addition to John who states that he was there, it is not clear who the women actually were; for with the exception of Mary of Magdala, included by all the Gospels, the "other women" present at the cross have different names in each Gospel. For John, Jesus' mother is the focus of his account of the crucifixion and the only woman who really counts. John does mention the two others crucified with him but gives no detail, as if this were a minor point.

Then he tells us Jesus other two words, "I am thirsty," and, "It is finished." "I thirst" is certainly more of an indication of Jesus' true humanity (to thirst) than John indicates elsewhere in his Gospel where he focuses more upon Jesus' divine nature. "It is finished" is so right for John's gospel, in which Jesus came with a mission and throughout his ministry, was always aware of that mission: to restore the broken relationship between God and God's children. In Jesus' death that mission has been finished.

Chapter Thirty-Four

Burial of Jesus

The Romans wanted the crucified bodies to hang there until they rotted away as an object lesson to others. Normally that would have been how Jesus death ended. However, because it was THE highest Jewish holiday and Rome was sensitive to the religious sentiments and observances of its subjects, Pilate allowed the removal of the bodies before sunset as Jewish law required. A normal crucifixion might last two days before death occurred.

All four Gospels agree that Joseph of Arimathea undertook the burial of Jesus. Matthew says simply that he was a rich man (27:57) and a follower of Jesus; Luke goes further, telling us, *"Now there was a good and righteous man named Joseph, who, though a member of the council had not agreed to their plan and action. He came from the Jewish town of Arimathea, and he was waiting expectantly for the kingdom of God. This man went to Pilate and asked for the body of Jesus. Then he took it down, wrapped it in a linen cloth, and laid it in a rock-hewn tomb where no one had ever been laid."* (23:50–56)

Mark gives us the most complete account: *"When evening had come, and since it was the day of Preparation, that is, the day before the Sabbath, Joseph of Arimathea, a respected member of the council, who was also himself waiting expectantly for the kingdom of God, went boldly to Pilate and asked for the body of Jesus. Then Pilate wondered if he were already dead; and summoning the centurion, he asked him whether he had been dead for some time. When he learned from the centurion that he was dead, he granted the body to Joseph. Then Joseph bought a linen cloth, and taking down the body, wrapped it in the linen cloth, and laid it in a tomb that had been hewn out of the rock. He then rolled a stone against the door of the tomb. Mary Magdalene and Mary the mother of Joses saw where the body was laid."* (15: 42-47)

John adds that Nicodemus, another member of the Sanhedrin, was with him. (9:39-40) Luke adds that no one had used the tomb previously. Mark stresses the courage of Joseph in approaching Pilate to ask for the body. Pilate is surprised Jesus is already dead; but if we consider how Jesus collapsed on the way to Golgotha and how stressed he had been the whole previous week; he was at the physical limits of endurance by the time the nails were driven.

Exactly where the town of Arimathea was is uncertain. It may have been a suburb of Jerusalem, may have been further away than that; but as a member of the council, while Joseph was a resident of Arimathea, he was at least a part time resident of Jerusalem. The fact that it was more than a casual part-time residency seems reasonable from the fact that he had a rock-hewn tomb outside the city. John adds that it was in a garden close to the place of crucifixion. Mark and Matthew both say the tomb was carved into the hillside. When the women arrived on Easter morning they had to look up, which would agree with the tomb being on a hillside. Although these are very small points, they show us the early tradition knew Jesus had been buried in a particular tomb.

Joseph and Nicodemus remove the body from the cross, place it in the tomb and have a stone rolled over the entrance, which was a common practice to protect from animals. Most likely, we can envision a groove cut into the bottom of the rock at the entrance to the tomb, providing a kind of track on which a grindstone-style rock was rolled in front of the tomb entrance. This would take more than one person--and men with great strength at that--to roll the stone once it was in place. Matthew, however, seems to think of the stone as a boulder, on which he says the angel could sit. Note Mark says Mary Magdalene and Mary the wife of Joses were at the burial and saw the location of the tomb, so they know where to come when they return later with spices.   John contradicts that, saying Joseph and Nicodemus brought with them a hundred pounds of myrrh to anoint the body. Mark and Matthew say nothing about spices.

Now, many modern critics doubt the entire burial story, saying Jesus' body was cast into the common grave of criminals along with the other two. This was the common way to get rid of the bodies, and yet all four Gospels unite in insisting some of his followers buried Jesus. The earliest tradition definitively insists on this, and there is no reason to agree with the critics on this point. Jesus died and was buried. Matthew's story, however, about the sealing of the tomb by Pilate and putting guards before the tomb is certainly suspect, perhaps added by Matthew to be evidence against the Jewish accusation that the disciples stole his body. Even more improbable is Matthew's assertion that the soldiers fell asleep and that the Jewish authorities bribed them! The penalty for falling asleep on the job if you were a Roman soldier was death with no reprieve.

After claiming the body of Jesus, Joseph of Arimathea takes the corpse down from the cross, wraps it in a linen cloth and lays it in his own tomb. Only John mentions that Nicodemus, who had previously encountered Jesus, also helped with Jesus' burial (19:39), a small point, but most likely it would have taken two to do it. The Gospels relate all this to show that two highly regarded men, of authentic Jewish faith, were witnesses to both the death and burial of Jesus. This pushed aside those who said Jesus did not really die. It was of extreme importance in the early church to make it clear Jesus was human, suffered, died, and was buried.

The disciples of Jesus, who should have been there to do all these things for their Lord, are not there. They deserted him, ran from him, and gathered behind locked doors, fearing they might be next.

What does happen next is in Part 6

Part Six

The Resurrection Narratives

Chapter Thirty-Five

Resurrection in Paul

The resurrection of Jesus is the pivotal point in the Christian faith. If it had not happened there would be no Christianity, it would have simply merged into the many religious cults of the first century. To understand what happened, we will begin with the earliest written account of the resurrection in Paul's letter to the Corinthians, then the four canonical Gospels, and finally Acts, which is really a continuation of Luke's Gospel.

The first account of the resurrection is in Paul's first letter to the Corinthians: *For I handed on to you as of first importance what I in turn had received: that Christ died for our sins in accordance with the scriptures, and that he was buried, and that he was raised on the third day in accordance with the scriptures, and that he appeared to Cephas, then to the twelve. Then he appeared to more than five hundred brothers and sisters at one time, most of whom are still alive, though some have died. Then he appeared to James, then to all the apostles. Last of all, as to one untimely born, he appeared also to me. For I am the least of the apostles, unfit to be called an apostle, because I persecuted the church of God. But by the grace of God I am what I am, and his grace toward me has not been in vain.* (15; 3-8)

It is worth noting that missing from this list are all the primary resurrection appearances in the Gospels--to the women in Jerusalem, to the eleven disciples behind locked doors in Jerusalem, to those same disciples with Thomas, to the two disciples on the road to Emmaus, to Mary Magdalene, and to the seven disciples who were fishing in Galilee. We will look at those later, but Paul's account of his experience predates all the resurrection appearances in the Gospels. As Paul relates it, it was not a bodily Jesus who appeared, but a vision, a spiritual experience. The whole idea of a bodily resurrection in the sense of a resuscitated corpse is strongly repudiated by Paul. He says flesh and blood have no place in God's kingdom and that the resurrected body of Jesus was a body of totally new attributes, nothing like his physical body. And yet Paul insisted again and again that it was in every way equal to the appearances of Jesus which the disciples experienced, apparently meaning those disciples he mentions in 1Corinthians.

So in distinction to the Gospel accounts, the earliest resurrection appearance is of a "spiritual body," not a physical body. Paul develops this in more detail in 1Corinthians15:35-50, where he is attempting to define what a believer's resurrection will be like: (adapted)

> .....(thus) it is with the resurrection of the dead. It is sown a physical body, it is raised a spiritual body. What I am saying, brothers and sisters, is this: flesh and blood cannot inherit the kingdom of God, nor does the perishable inherit the imperishable.

Paul's personal experience and his statements in Corinthians strongly imply Jesus' resurrection in a spiritual body is what was known and believed in the early church, barely 10-15 years after the event had occurred. Only a few years later, by the time Matthew and Luke are writing, more substantial and substantially more satisfying appearances are being recorded. We turn to those next.

In his Emmaus story, Luke said that when the two men return to Jerusalem to tell the others what had happened, before they can speak, the disciples tell them, "The Lord has risen ...and he appeared to Simon." Except for Paul's list above and this one sentence in Luke, there is no mention of Jesus appearing to Peter anywhere else in the New Testament, not even in Mark whose Gospel is based upon Peter. Why Peter is so lightly mentioned is one of the mysteries of manuscript tradition.

Chapter Thirty-Six

Resurrection in Mark

Mark is the earliest Gospel and, to our surprise, it tells of the resurrection only by recounting an empty tomb. There are no appearances of a risen Jesus in Mark. This is Mark's resurrection account (16:1-8):

> When the Sabbath was over, Mary Magdalene, and Mary the mother of James, and Salome bought spices, so that they might go and anoint him. And very early on the first day of the week, when the sun had risen, they went to the tomb. They had been saying to one another, "Who will roll away the stone for us from the entrance to the tomb?" When they looked up, they saw that the stone, which was very large, had already been rolled back. As they entered the tomb, they saw a young man, dressed in a white robe, sitting on the right side; and they were alarmed. But he said to them, "Do not be alarmed; you are looking for Jesus of Nazareth, who was crucified. He has been raised; he is not here. Look, there is the place they laid him. But go, tell his disciples and Peter that he is going ahead of you to Galilee; there you will see him, just as he told you." So they went out and fled from the tomb, for terror and amazement had seized them; and they said nothing to anyone, for they were afraid.

This is the first statement of the empty tomb. A young man is there, dressed in a white robe. Is this an angel or is it possibly Mark himself? Mark's Gospel tells us that in the garden of Gethsemane, "A certain young man was following him, wearing nothing but a linen cloth. They caught hold of him, but he left the linen cloth and ran off naked." (14: 51-52) It is an interesting possibility that this young man in the tomb was that same young man. The Greek word "neaniskos" (young man) is used only twice in the New Testament: in the garden on the night of Jesus' arrest, and at the tomb in Mark.

It is an exciting thought that young Mark, son of the woman whose home was used for the Last Supper, followed them from there to Gethsemane and was still with them when the soldiers came. All we know for sure is that the young man in the garden ran away. Nothing more is said of him; but reasonable surmise would allow him to remain involved in the community, perhaps be present at the crucifixion, and then make his way to the tomb. Finding it empty, he is sitting there when the women come. What Mark's Gospel does tell us is that on Sunday morning, less than 48 hours after the death of Jesus, the women come to anoint his body and a young man is sitting there. He tells them, "Jesus is risen," and sends them to inform the disciples. Then Mark ends with the ominous words.... "They told no one for they were afraid!"

While Mark's ending seems to have been accepted in the early community, a generation later it ran into difficulty because it contained no actual appearance of the risen Jesus. We find in various copies that other endings were added to rectify the original. The first, called the "shorter ending," was so obviously not written in the style of Mark and presented Jesus in a way so unlike Mark, that it was never accepted and quickly dropped out of use. It is in none of the earliest manuscripts, but we still have it in some translations.

And all that had been commanded them they told briefly
to those around Peter. And afterward Jesus himself sent

out through them, from east to west, the sacred and im-
perishable proclamation of eternal salvation.

The second effort, which added to Chapter 16, verses 9-19, was instantly popular in the later church and was included in Jerome's Latin translation, "The Vulgate." Jerome's Bible was written about 400 and was for centuries the official Roman Catholic Bible and thus the official Bible of the whole church. This second ending was also included in the King James Version of the Bible in 1611. During this time the longer ending gained many supporters.

However, the evidence is clear; Mark ended his Gospel at 16:8. Neither of the added endings is in our earliest and most reliable Greek copies of Mark. When scholars use those critical tools we discussed earlier, it is quickly evident that the author took sections of the endings of Matthew, Luke and John and wove them together. The manuscript evidence also determines it is an obvious creation from a somewhat later time in the community. So the original ending of Mark **is** the original ending; and when added to what Paul has said, presents us with an interesting situation as we consider the resurrection appearances in the later Gospels!

Mark says that on the last night of Jesus' life after supper he told the disciples, "But after I am raised up, I will go before you to Galilee." (14:28) Then he ends his Gospel with the empty tomb, fear in the women's' hearts, and no bodily appearance of Jesus. Mark understands Jesus as having ascended to the Father in his resurrection and therefore could not appear in the flesh, as the other Gospels will later relate. There is no ascension either in Mark, for the same reason.

Mark's Gospel does not end in obvious triumph and victory with a physical resurrection appearance of Jesus. This is hard to understand until we realize Mark is writing for the church barely 20 years after the resurrection. If there had been appearances of Jesus in the manner in which Matthew and Luke relate, it is doubtful Mark would have ignored them. It seems most likely the resurrection experiences of Jesus in the early community were that of a more spiritual body.

Mark ends his Gospel with three women fleeing from the tomb with trembling and terror. In spite of the fact that in that era women were not credible witnesses, Mark says it was three women who first witnessed the empty tomb. They speak to no one because of their fear. And perhaps because they knew no one would believe them anyhow. The young man at the tomb commanded them to tell Peter and the disciples to go to Galilee, where they would see Jesus. (Mark16: 6) These words clearly point back to the promise of Jesus in Mark where Jesus said he would meet with the disciples in Galilee after his resurrection. (14: 28)

When Mark's gospel is judged from a literary perspective, the ending is powerful, striking, and hits just the right note. As the women stood before the empty tomb and the young man in a white robe tells them Jesus has risen, is not silence, terror, and abject fear a reasonable response? I think so, and we can almost hear the women saying to each other, "... My God, what now?"

From the viewpoint of a theological analysis, perhaps Mark does not include appearances of the risen Jesus because he is saying that, then as now, everybody gets the same experience of the resurrection--not the appearance of a physical body walking around, but the same spiritual certainty as Paul, not only that Jesus has been resurrected but that he has come to us. And thank you, Holy Spirit, because of your witness to us, we know in a manner beyond understanding that this is so.

Chapter Thirty-Seven

Resurrection in Matthew

As Matthew presents his resurrection story, he first copies from Mark, then adds to it: (Matt 28:1-20)

After the Sabbath, as the first day of the week was dawning, Mary Magdalene and the other Mary went to see the tomb. And suddenly there was a great earthquake; for an angel of the Lord, descending from heaven, came and rolled back the stone and sat on it. His appearance was like lightning and his clothing white as snow. For fear of him the guards shook and became like dead men. But the angel said to the women, "Do not be afraid; I know that you are looking for Jesus who was crucified. He is not here; for he has been raised, as he said. Come; see the place where he lay. Then go quickly and tell his disciples, 'He has been raised from the dead, and indeed he is going ahead of you to Galilee; there you will see him.' This is my message for you." So they left the tomb quickly with fear and great joy, and ran to tell his disciples. Suddenly Jesus met them and said, "Greetings!" And they came to him, took hold of his feet, and worshiped him. Then Jesus said to them, "Do not be afraid; go and tell my brothers to go

*to Galilee; there they will see me." While they were go-
ing, some of the guard went into the city and told the chief
priests everything that had happened. After the priests
had assembled with the elders, they devised a plan to give
a large sum of money to the soldiers, telling them, "You
must say, 'His disciples came by night and stole him away
while we were asleep.' If this comes to the governor's
ears, we will satisfy him and keep you out of trouble." So
they took the money and did as they were directed. And
this story is still told among the Jews to this day."*

Compared to Mark, does not Matthew's account seem somewhat fanciful? He adds an earthquake to the story to make it clear a big deal is
happening. The young man in Mark becomes an angel, and rather than
sitting in the tomb, he has rolled away the stone and is sitting on it. Unlike
Mark, Matthew leaves out Salome and the women do not remain silent,
but report to the disciples. By adding that squadron of guards to be witnesses to what happened, Matthew neatly counters the rumor that the
disciples stole his body. And then, a kind of thumb in the eye to religious
leaders, he says they bribed the guards to lie! Matthew must have then
realized that any Roman soldier who fell asleep on duty faced death, no
excuses accepted. He has to get them out of that spot, so in verse 14 he
has the religious leaders say they will protect the soldiers from Pilate.

It is difficult to accept most of this as historical. First, the Jewish leaders would never have gone to Pilate on the Sabbath, nor would they have
given any credence to the third day story in the first place. Pilate certainly
would not have given it a thought, if he even knew of it, which is not
very probable. Had this whole incident actually taken place, considering
Pilate's personal opinion that Jesus was innocent, he likely would have
dug in his heels and said, "No Guards. The man is dead, you got what
you wanted."

Matthew moves quickly to Galilee, to the mountain "to which Jesus
had directed them" and says a startling thing, "When they saw him, they

worshiped him; but some doubted."(28:17). How could anyone doubt a resurrected, physically present Jesus? Matthew is writing late in the tradition when he finishes his resurrection account by having Jesus tell the disciples to use a baptismal formula that came into the church only in much later years: *And Jesus came and said to them, "All authority in heaven and on earth has been given to me. Go therefore and make disciples of all nations, baptizing them in the name of the Father and of the Son and of the Holy Spirit, and teaching them to obey everything that I have commanded you. And remember, I am with you always, to the end of the age." (28; 19)*

It is not likely Jesus would have uttered those words. For at least two generations the community had baptized only "in the name of Jesus." It is possible Matthew changes that to underscore the commitment of the community to Gentiles, which had been such a point of contention between James and Paul in Jerusalem a generation earlier.

In conclusion, while Matthew's account may not be historically accurate in all aspects, it is undeniably true in the deepest and most essential sense: Jesus had been raised from the dead by the power of God.

Chapter Thirty-Eight

Resurrection in Luke

The account of Jesus' resurrection in the Gospel of Luke is the longest of the four Gospels. (24:1-53)

But on the first day of the week, at early dawn, they came to the tomb, taking the spices that they had prepared. They found the stone rolled away from the tomb, but when they went in, they did not find the body. While they were perplexed about this, suddenly two men in dazzling clothes stood beside them. The women were terrified and bowed their faces to the ground, but the men said to them, "Why do you look for the living among the dead? He is not here, but has risen. Remember how he told you, while he was still in Galilee, that the Son of Man must be handed over to sinners, and be crucified, and on the third day rise again." Then they remembered his words, and returning from the tomb, they told all this to the eleven and to all the rest. Now it was Mary Magdalene, Joanna, Mary the mother of James, and the other women with them who told this to the apostles. But these words seemed to them an idle tale, and they did not believe them. But Peter got up and ran to the tomb; stooping and looking in, he saw the linen cloths by themselves; then he went home, amazed at what had happened.

While copying Mark's bare bones account, Luke modifies Mark's single young man at the tomb into two men, likely because Jewish law required two male witnesses to be a credible report. Like Matthew, Luke also omits Salome from Mark's account, but he adds Joanna and Mary, the mother of James. Once again, as in Mark, the women come wondering who would roll away the stone. It was rolled away in Mark, and Luke continues with that approach, unlike Matthew, who answered the women's question with an earthquake and an angel descending from heaven to roll the stone away.

Matthew's resurrection appearances take place in Judea, none in Galilee, as are reported by Mark and Luke. Apparently there were two groups of resurrection appearances remembered in the early church; one taking place in and around Jerusalem, the other in Galilee. The tomb, of course, was in Jerusalem, so all the Gospel accounts begin in Jerusalem and all include women or a woman going to the tomb. (Luke 24: 6)

It was Paul's view that the resurrection changed Jesus' body into a new and glorious body, not subject to any of the constraints of this physical world: *"The Lord Jesus Christ, by the power that enables Him to subject all things to Himself, will transform our lowly bodies to be like His glorious body."* (Philippians 3:21) Luke traveled with Paul for at least a year and most likely they would have discussed all of this. However, while Luke adopted Paul's position, he adapted it so Jesus' physical body was also able to materialize and de-materialize at will, requiring it to be in some manner a spiritual body as well.

This dual understanding is also evident in Luke's beautiful Emmaus story. (24:13-35) Although almost certainly based upon an actual incident, it is polished by Luke into a truly wonderful story, a perfectly constructed narrative of the risen Christ experienced by two men on the way home from Jerusalem to Emmaus. Luke says one of the men was Cleopas, a name mentioned nowhere else in the New Testament; but if Luke meant to say Clopas, then we have a neat anchoring into history. Clopas was Jesus' uncle by marriage, the husband of Jesus' mother's sister, and the father of Simeon, who succeeded James as the leader of the church in Jerusalem.

If Luke meant Clopas, which is quite likely, this little story is one of the most important in the early tradition. Then the wedding in Cana was in Mary's family, probably that of her sister, explaining why Mary takes such an active part in the wedding. Clopas, the husband of Mary's sister, then becomes the host of the wedding at which water becomes wine. Would not the resurrected Jesus seek out his uncle, who could well have been an important part of his life after Joseph died? This is assumption, since we do not know the age of Jesus when Joseph died, but what a great possibility. The other man on the walk, not named, could be Simeon, Jesus' cousin. Whatever the family involvement may or may not have been Luke's story had tremendous importance in the early church.

However, the important part of the story is that, when Jesus joins them, Luke says their eyes are "prevented" from recognizing him. I think they were deep in depression, and not expecting Jesus, they did not see him. All hope was gone. They were in grief; and if you have ever been in grief or know someone in grief, often nothing going on registers. People say things and do things; but those in grief are "prevented" from either hearing or seeing it, and often they do not even remember it. Clopas and his companion in Luke's story compare to John's story of Mary Magdalene at the tomb, who at first did not recognize Jesus either, thinking him to be the gardener.

The two men on the way to Emmaus do not recognize Jesus; but he has told them such amazing stuff, that when they get home and Jesus is about to leave, they "constrain" him. In other words, they insist that he stay for supper. It is when he broke the bread and blessed it, that their eyes are opened; they remember other times, other occasions, when Jesus had done that. Possibly, especially if it is Clopas and Simeon, they had been at the Last Supper. Anyhow, they recognize him and he vanishes. Luke's story gives us what is a physical or bodily appearance of Jesus; yet, as he "vanishes," it suggests it was not a normal bodily appearance.

But then the two men, having returned to Jerusalem, while they are still meeting with the disciples (Luke says "while they were still talking"),

Jesus appears again. "They thought they were seeing a Ghost," Luke says, once again suggesting a non-physical body. Or maybe not. Jesus says, "Look at my hands and my feet. It is I myself. Touch me and see, for a spirit does not have flesh and bones as you see here." Then, when the disciples still hesitate, Jesus asks, "Have you anything to eat?" (24:39-40) Luke makes it clear Jesus is not a ghost; the resurrection of Jesus is utterly real, not imagined; and Jesus is not just a spirit but the complete Jesus.

Then Luke continues with the ascension. The ascension is an outlier in the early tradition. Paul, Mark, John and Matthew insist the resurrection and ascension are a single event; Jesus resurrected and ascended simultaneously.

So who is right? We need to look at St. John before we attempt to answer that!

Chapter Thirty-Nine

Resurrection in John

John 20:1-31 is John's version of the resurrection. (We will consider John 21 separately.) John has two distinctive appearances. The first is the well-known story of Mary at the tomb:

> *Early on the first day of the week, while it was still dark, Mary Magdalene came to the tomb and saw that the stone had been removed from the tomb. So she ran and went to Simon Peter and the other disciple, the one whom Jesus loved, and said to them, "They have taken the Lord out of the tomb, and we do not know where they have laid him." Then Peter and the other disciple set out and went toward the tomb. The two were running together, but the other disciple outran Peter and reached the tomb first. He bent down to look in and saw the linen wrappings lying there, but he did not go in. Then Simon Peter came, following him, and went into the tomb. He saw the linen wrappings lying there, and the cloth that had been on Jesus' head, not lying with the linen wrappings but rolled up in a place by itself. Then the other disciple, who reached the tomb first, also went in, and he saw and believed; for as yet they did not understand the scripture, that he must rise from the dead. Then the disciples returned to their homes. (But) Mary stood weeping outside the tomb. As she wept, she*

bent over to look into the tomb; and she saw two angels in white, sitting where the body of Jesus had been lying, one at the head and the other at the feet. They said to her, "Woman, why are you weeping?" She said to them, "They have taken away my Lord, and I do not know where they have laid him." When she had said this, she turned around and saw Jesus standing there, but she did not know that it was Jesus. Jesus said to her, "Woman, why are you weeping? Whom are you looking for?" Supposing him to be the gardener, she said to him, "Sir, if you have carried him away, tell me where you have laid him, and I will take him away." Jesus said to her, "Mary!" She turned and said to him in Hebrew "Rabbouni!" (which means Teacher)? Jesus said to her, "Do not hold on to me, because I have not yet ascended to the Father. But go to my brothers and say to them, 'I am ascending to my Father and your Father, to my God and your God.'" Mary Magdalene went and announced to the disciples, "I have seen the Lord"; and she told them that he had said these things to her.

This account is only in John's gospel. It is the first appearance of Jesus in the gospel accounts, and it is to Mary. Place that into the context of the importance of women in Jesus' ministry and his apparent special relationship to Mary, and this is a truly beautiful and tender story. Just as the disciples on the road to Emmaus, Mary does not recognize Jesus. Jesus never appeared to anyone but his disciples, and even they needed some special connection, some word or act, in order to recognize him. Is this John telling us that it is in the words and deeds of the worshipping community that we too meet the risen Lord? That seems to be the case for John tells us that Jesus says to Mary, "Do not hold on to me." Oh, how she wanted to hold him, hold on to him! But he explains why..."I have not yet ascended to the Father." Post-resurrection our union with Jesus, his presence with us, is no longer physical but spiritual. It must be so, for as

Paul so succinctly puts it, mortal bodies, flesh and blood, cannot comprehend the Kingdom that is God's. (1Corinthians 15:50) Not only Mary but Clopas and all the disciples would have held on to him for dear life if they could have! That was not possible…he was about to ascend to his Father and our Father.

The Thomas episode is another story unique to John and it presents a possible complication to the timing of the ascension.

When it was evening on that day, the first day of the week, and the doors of the house where the disciples had met were locked for fear of the Jews, Jesus came and stood among them and said, "Peace be with you." After he said this, he showed them his hands and his side. Then the disciples rejoiced when they saw the Lord." " Jesus said to them again, "Peace be with you. As the Father has sent me, so I send you." When he had said this, he breathed on them and said to them, "Receive the Holy Spirit. If you forgive the sins of any, they are forgiven them; if you retain the sins of any, they are retained." "But Thomas (who was called the Twin, one of the twelve, was not with them when Jesus came. So the other disciples told him, "We have seen the Lord." But he said to them, "Unless I see the mark of the nails in his hands, and put my finger in the mark of the nails and my hand in his side, I will not believe." A week later his disciples were again in the house, and Thomas was with them. Although the doors were shut, Jesus came and stood among them and said, "Peace be with you." Then he said to Thomas, "Put your finger here and see my hands. Reach out your hand and put it in my side. Do not doubt but believe." Thomas answered him, "My Lord and my God!" Jesus said to him, "Have you believed because you have seen me? Blessed are those who have not seen and yet have come to believe. (20: 19--29)

John seems to have ended this appearance of Jesus at verse 23: *"When he had said this, he breathed on them and said to them, 'Receive the Holy Spirit. If you forgive the sins of any, they are forgiven them; if you retain the sins of any, they are retained.'"* That seems a good place to stop, and we do not expect John to launch into another appearance story. Also, in verses 19-23, John does not say or even imply that any disciple is missing from that first meeting with Jesus. And how do we understand what Jesus says to Mary, "Tell the disciples I am ascending to the Father," when he then appears to Thomas in a very physical body? It is very strange, unless in pointing out the nail prints and saying, "Put your hand into my side," John is making it clear the crucified Jesus and the ascended Jesus is the same person--the whole, real Jesus has been raised, not just his spirit.

This does not contradict John's general approach, which follows Mark and Paul in maintaining Jesus ascended to the Father in his resurrection, and therefore all the appearances of Jesus are of a spiritual body, not a physical one. In the Thomas story, because Jesus has ascended to glory and appears in his glorified body, he is able to bestow the spirit upon them; and Thomas is able to make the statement, "My Lord and My God." That acclamation was never given to Jesus in the Gospels. Never is Jesus in any manner called "God," and Jesus repeatedly forbids the disciples from calling him anything approaching, "My Lord and my God." But now, since he is the ascended Jesus, the Christ of glory, this designation is not only apt, but correct. The risen, ascended Jesus is our Lord and our God.

The upper room story is of both theological and textual importance. It is of textual importance because John's account claims it was in this upper room that Jesus bestows the Holy Spirit. Luke says that takes place on the event of Pentecost. (Acts 2: 1-13) It is of theological importance because Thomas represents all who refuse to believe unless they see a miracle. Jesus says, *"Blessed are those who have not seen and yet have come to believe,"* which is John's way of agreeing with Mark and Paul that the appearances of Jesus have only a relative value. That is, the stories are not a substitute for a personal resurrection experience, the only valid evidence we should accept as definitive. John is saying that, as we live within the community of faith, as we share the Lord's Supper, we too have our own resurrection experiences of Jesus.

This makes the appearance to the disciples gathered in the upper room the fitting and proper end to the New Testament appearances of Jesus. If we had another dozen; and if we piled them one on another, the size of the pile, the number of appearances, would not make the resurrection any more true or real, so John ends his Gospel in Chapter 20, verses 30-31: *"Now Jesus did many other signs in the presence of his disciples, which are not written in this book. But these are written so that you may come to believe that Jesus is the Messiah, the Son of God, and that through believing you may have life in his name."*

◆ ◆ ◆

Then we have John's infamous Chapter 21! His Gospel ends perfectly at Chapter 20:31. The existence of Chapter 21 has caused a contentious New Testament debate. As far as we know, there is no copy of John's gospel without chapter 21, so that argues for it being written and intended by John. Yet the Gospel so obviously and beautifully ends at 20:31 that many efforts have tried to explain the additional chapter, either as a later second thought by John himself or as an addition by disciples of John. This theory is supported by that tantalizing statement in verse 24 of the epilog: "This *is the disciple who is testifying to these things and has written them, and we know that his testimony is true."* Does "we" refer to the disciples who added the chapter? There are many thoughts and theories about why this final chapter was added to John's Gospel but none can be completely substantiated. . Perhaps the best way to leave it is to say what Winston Churchill said concerning Russia during WWII: "…a riddle wrapped in a mystery inside an enigma."

Chapter Forty

What does it all mean?

In 1st Corinthians15 Paul states that if there is no resurrection life is nothing and all is in vain. Nevertheless, Paul is certain that Christ did rise, that it is a fact, it did happen. Then he goes on to say whether that fact means anything to us depends on whether or not we believe it. It has no meaning if we do not believe it.

Many cannot believe it because the revival of a corpse after three days is scientifically very improbable. Even common sense, usually given the more scientific title of "analogy," tells us that the same physical laws govern life today that governed life in the past; so since the dead do not rise today, they did not rise then. Therefore Jesus did not rise either. This argument, rather smugly asserted for generations, is no longer an argument which should be heard from scientists today, for now we live in a quantum world where impossible things happen every moment. In the quantum world of chance and chaos and probability there is no reason why God could not have changed the rules and decided to bring about a new creation in which the old rules no longer apply.

Quarks occupy two different places at the same time. Light travels in waves or in particles, whichever you want; it will, literally, do what you ask of it. Time is circular or perhaps nonexistent. Parallel universes are a reasonable hypothesis. To quantum science the best definition of impossible is simply that which we do not yet understand. That is also a good theological assessment of Jesus' resurrection; God began a new law of nature in which the dead do rise; and as Paul put it, Jesus is the first to do so.

Nonetheless, we need to be clear from the start that so called "scientific evidence" will not prove the resurrection. God simply does not work through objective experience. Angels do not descend from the sky. Voices do not thunder from heaven. God works always through Elijah's inner "'still small voice" and therefore we can expect that the resurrection appearances of Jesus would come in the same way, not as supernatural or objective realities, but personal subjective experiences. If the disciples had had a video camera, there would have been nothing to record. And even if there were a video recording, it would make no difference; skeptics would still be skeptics, doubters would still have doubt. As Jesus said, even someone returning from the dead would not prove anything; we would continue to hold to our prejudices or certainties. So other than the witness of the Spirit to each of us personally, the only proof we have of the resurrection is the witness of the Gospel accounts we have looked at, which claim the risen Jesus appeared to them. We have stories telling us what the early community experienced. We do not have video tapes. Now would they likely prove anything if we did.

What can be proven by reasonable historical sources is that Jesus was crucified. What cannot be proven, except through the Holy Spirit, is the meaning of his crucifixion: that by the grace of God the death of Jesus is also MY death. And the Resurrection of Jesus is also my resurrection. When we are in Christ, we are a new creation, the old is gone; it is no longer who we are, for we have died to this temporal existence and are already living in God's kingdom. Jesus' resurrection is not merely an event long in the past; it is also a present reality, for as God raised Jesus to new life, so God raises us to new life.

Modern physics' theory of "quantum entanglement" is a way of stating this in a 21st century manner. Quantum entanglement tells us that when two particles interact, they become entangled, each individual particle "mixed" with that of the other. From that moment on the two could be separated to different ends of the universe but they would remain completely connected with each other. What each "was" is no longer what it "is," for they are now joined together; they are a new creation. So also the Gospels tell us when we are willing to become one with Christ, and thus one with God, we are immediately brought into the "kingdom." Living in eternity, past, present, and future are now only words describing a small part of our reality, not the whole of it.

Thus the point of this book is that, as we read the New Testament, we must do so with the eyes of faith. People of faith wrote the New Testament--the entire Bible--to be read by people of faith. Faith is the whole and necessary ingredient to understanding the Word of God. It sounds strange to say it, but unless we believe Jesus is raised, we cannot believe Jesus is raised. Until we are in love, we are not in love. Then when we are, how and why it happened takes on mythical and wondrous proportions. As the song says, "Love changes everything." It may not change us enough, and we remain unworthy of being loved, and yet love is given to us. That is concisely what the New Testament is telling us about our relationship with God in Jesus.

In the 21st century the worldview with which we live each day is in almost every respect different, not only from the 1st century, but from any age before us. It is a world of aggressive secularism, half-truths and distortions, scientific theories presented as absolute truths, the implicit assumption being that God is dead and life is without meaning. The 21st century worldview is that true reality is a life freed of the shackles of religion, in which there is no longer any need of the "God hypothesis." (Stephen Hawking and Leonard Mlodinow, "The Grand Design") So it goes, and for the most part it goes unchallenged. It is useless to argue the point, because the secular worldview simply does not have the ability to understand the things of God. It does not have the "eyes to see," as Jesus put it--something which only comes as a gift of God to the community of faith and can only be understood within the community of faith.

To be clear, the resurrection as an historical event did happen in Palestine about the year 32. That event is told in the New Testament resurrection appearances of Jesus. Those appearance stories—not the Resurrection of Jesus itself, but the accounts of it--are equally as metaphorical and mythical as they are historical. This must be, because what happened in Jesus' resurrection is more than his body resuscitated, and faith in the resurrection is so much more than merely believing in a series of appearances of Jesus.

What happened in the resurrection is what happens whenever the community gathers in fellowship, and as we share each Lord's Supper, we know, as they knew, Jesus is with us. It is not imagination. It is the deepest most real of spiritual reality. So it was for the disciples, not just the eleven, but all of them—men, women, Jews, Gentiles, the whole fellowship. When they gathered, and remembered, Jesus was there with them, and whatever it was they actually experienced, they were the only ones who had the resurrection experience! There are no appearances to anyone outside the circle of friends and family of Jesus. He appeared to no one outside the fellowship of faith. It would have been useless to do so.

There is no question it is mysterious, but only those who respond to the call of the Spirit come to understand. Doubt consumes those, who rather than respond, simply stand aside and wonder. That is true whether at the foot of the cross that crucifixion day or any day since then. As long as one keeps examining the facts, looking for some definite proof, demanding certainty before believing, there will never be more than doubt. Doubt is all there can be, because "certainty" is merely a code word for understanding something on our own terms. The desire for certainty supposes that "our own terms" is the measure of truth and veracity and that there is no reality other than what we can define or understand in our own minds. "Our own minds" then becomes the measure for all that is real and true.

It is the witness of the New Testament that belief in the incarnation, and in the resurrection, comes through the Holy Spirit as a gift. God communicates with each of us personally, through an inner spiritual reality, and an outward fellowship of faith which affirms that experience. The

Holy Spirit comes to us, reaches through our foolish self-reliance, and brings us into the fellowship we call the church. Then and now, Jesus comes only to believers. It is indeed, as Mark so stunningly tells us, that God does not work through objective means, does not overwhelm us with evidence, but always leaves room for another interpretation.

Whenever the Spirit comes there is always another way to under-stand what happened. In whatever way the risen Jesus came to the disciples, in a resurrection appearance of an entirely different dimension and quality than our experience or in the same manner he comes to us; either way, the miracle remains! In Jesus' resurrection death has been abolished. Ended. Overcome. For the early community of believers, how-ever they experienced it, the resurrection was so real and certain they could do nothing else but shout to the whole world the triumphant Easter cry: "He is Risen!"

It is the dramatic and incredible assertion of the entire New Testament that Jesus lives; and because Jesus lives, we too shall live. When it comes to the exact how, why and what of the Resurrection, the Gospels did their best; but in the end, the true intention of their accounts is to tell us, as historian Martin Marty put it, to "just sing "Hallelujah!" (Washington Post "On Faith" April 8 2007)

Soli deo Gloria!

Postscript

From the very beginning of human development we have been faced with a choice...is the universe rational or not? Do things make sense? Seventeenth century rationalism and the view of life termed classical materialism dominated the culture and religion of much of the world until the late 20th century. The uncovering of a microscopic world and a new physics called quantum mechanics brought new and exciting concepts of reality, even as material realism continued to hang around like a drunk after a party, stumbling around in a stupor, refusing to leave.

But it is understandable; after 300 years of absolute certainty that life was a product of cause and effect--one thing causing and therefore leading to another--to be suddenly thrust into a world of quarks and quasars, black holes and time warps, red giants and white dwarfs, string theory and chaos, alternative universes and big bang evolution, chaos, purposelessness and meaninglessness are enough to make anyone's eyes begin to blur.

And they should, for science confidently describes its view of reality as new insight, even as it understands less about the deepest or truest reality than the first century world. When asked the most essential questions of existence, the ones answered in the metaphors and images of the New Testament, science hesitates, fumbles around a bit, then begins to mumble about alternate universes, multi universes, and finally shrugs and says "...it is the business of science to measure, not to explain."

But that is not enough. It is an inadequate answer. But assuming it is THE answer, true believers become agnostics, marginal believers become atheists, humanists become cynics; all become caught in a kind of malaise of depression and uncertainty. And the cry goes out, "Who cares if it's random meaninglessness anyhow?" We long for Newton's falling apple or Einstein's rushing train! These are metaphors we can understand, even if they are not on the same level as water changed into wine, walking on water, blind men seeing, or the creation story in Genesis.

I dare to hope this little book may help us to, as Luke says, "Repent, and turn back, so that your sins may be wiped away, that times of refreshing may come from the presence of the Lord, and that He may send Jesus, the Christ, who has been appointed for you". (Acts 3: 19, 20)

The End

About the Author

Wayne R. Viereck has been a pastor for Lutheran congregations for forty-five years. He spent five years with the Community Church at Saddlebrooke in Tucson, Arizona, and is currently serving part time at the Resurrection Lutheran Church in Tucson.

Viereck received his bachelor's degree from the University of Wisconsin and his master's degree from the Lutheran School of Theology at Chicago. He also earned a doctorate in ministry.

During his fifty-five years in the ministry, Viereck heard the same questions—questions he himself wrestled with as a seminary student—coming up time and again from members of his congregation. His new book, *Then Is Now*, is an exploration of some of these questions and the answers the New Testament provides.

Made in the USA
San Bernardino, CA
20 January 2018